DEDICATION

THIS HISTORY OF TWICKENHAM IS DEDICATED
TO THE TOWN AND ITS RESIDENTS:
PAST, PRESENT AND FUTURE.

TWICKENHAM
A HISTORY & CELEBRATION

HAZELLE JACKSON

THE FRANCIS FRITH COLLECTION

www.francisfrith.co.uk

First published in the United Kingdom in 2005
by The Francis Frith Collection®

Hardback Edition 2005
ISBN 1-84589-220-8

British Library Cataloguing in Publication Data

Twickenham - A History & Celebration
Hazelle Jackson

The Francis Frith Collection
Frith's Barn, Teffont,
Salisbury, Wiltshire SP3 5QP
Tel: +44 (0) 1722 716 376
Email: info@francisfrith.co.uk
www.francisfrith.co.uk

Printed and bound in England

Front Cover: **TWICKENHAM, KING STREET 1909** T9100lt

Additional modern photographs by Hazelle Jackson.

Domesday extract used in timeline by kind permission of
Alecto Historical Editions, www.domesdaybook.org
Aerial photographs reproduced under licence from
Simmons Aerofilms Limited.
Historical Ordnance Survey maps reproduced under licence from
Homecheck.co.uk

Every attempt has been made to contact copyright holders of
illustrative material. We will be happy to give full acknowledgement in
future editions for any items not credited. Any information should be
directed to The Francis Frith Collection.

*The colour-tinting in this book is for illustrative purposes only,
and is not intended to be historically accurate*

AS WITH ANY HISTORICAL DATABASE, THE FRANCIS FRITH
ARCHIVE IS CONSTANTLY BEING CORRECTED AND
IMPROVED, AND THE PUBLISHERS WOULD WELCOME
INFORMATION ON OMISSIONS OR INACCURACIES

CONTENTS

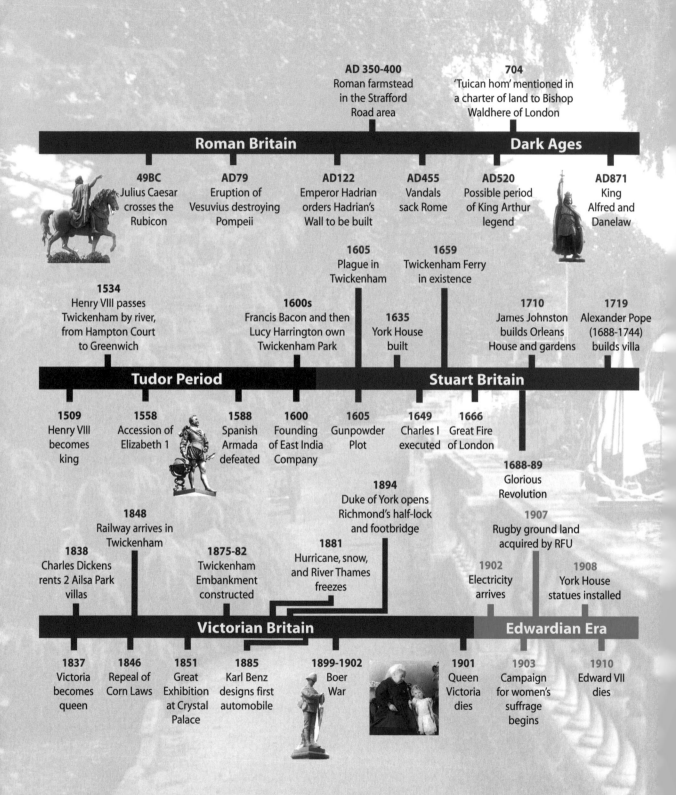

TWICKENHAM
A HISTORY & CELEBRATION

AD 350-400
Roman farmstead in the Strafford Road area

704
'Tuican hom' mentioned in a charter of land to Bishop Waldhere of London

Roman Britain

Dark Ages

49BC
Julius Caesar crosses the Rubicon

AD79
Eruption of Vesuvius destroying Pompeii

AD122
Emperor Hadrian orders Hadrian's Wall to be built

AD455
Vandals sack Rome

AD520
Possible period of King Arthur legend

AD871
King Alfred and Danelaw

1534
Henry VIII passes Twickenham by river, from Hampton Court to Greenwich

1600s
Francis Bacon and then Lucy Harrington own Twickenham Park

1605
Plague in Twickenham

1635
York House built

1659
Twickenham Ferry in existence

1710
James Johnston builds Orleans House and gardens

1719
Alexander Pope (1688-1744) builds villa

Tudor Period

Stuart Britain

1509
Henry VIII becomes king

1558
Accession of Elizabeth 1

1588
Spanish Armada defeated

1600
Founding of East India Company

1605
Gunpowder Plot

1649
Charles I executed

1666
Great Fire of London

1688-89
Glorious Revolution

1894
Duke of York opens Richmond's half-lock and footbridge

1907
Rugby ground land acquired by RFU

1848
Railway arrives in Twickenham

1875-82
Twickenham Embankment constructed

1881
Hurricane, snow, and River Thames freezes

1902
Electricity arrives

1908
York House statues installed

1838
Charles Dickens rents 2 Ailsa Park villas

Victorian Britain

Edwardian Era

1837
Victoria becomes queen

1846
Repeal of Corn Laws

1851
Great Exhibition at Crystal Palace

1885
Karl Benz designs first automobile

1899-1902
Boer War

1901
Queen Victoria dies

1903
Campaign for women's suffrage begins

1910
Edward VII dies

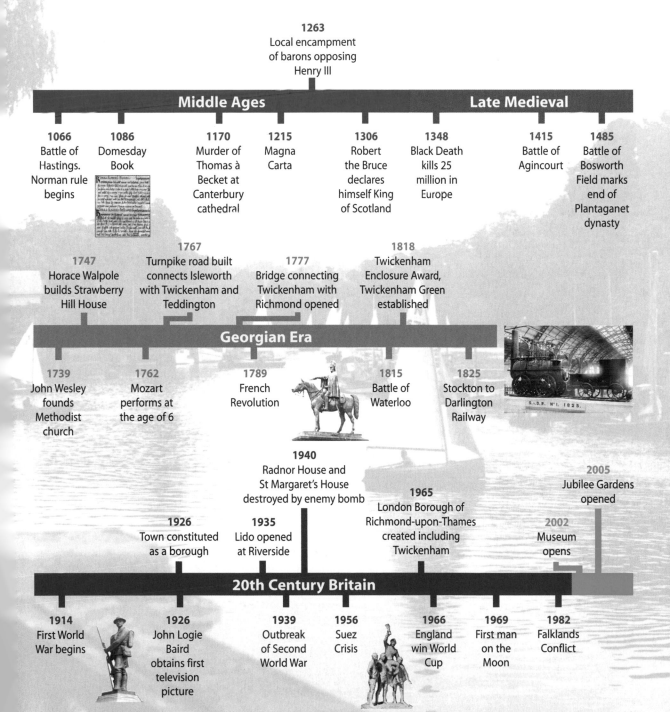

1263
Local encampment of barons opposing Henry III

Middle Ages

Late Medieval

1066
Battle of Hastings. Norman rule begins

1086
Domesday Book

1170
Murder of Thomas à Becket at Canterbury cathedral

1215
Magna Carta

1306
Robert the Bruce declares himself King of Scotland

1348
Black Death kills 25 million in Europe

1415
Battle of Agincourt

1485
Battle of Bosworth Field marks end of Plantaganet dynasty

1747
Horace Walpole builds Strawberry Hill House

1767
Turnpike road built connects Isleworth with Twickenham and Teddington

1777
Bridge connecting Twickenham with Richmond opened

1818
Twickenham Enclosure Award, Twickenham Green established

Georgian Era

1739
John Wesley founds Methodist church

1762
Mozart performs at the age of 6

1789
French Revolution

1815
Battle of Waterloo

1825
Stockton to Darlington Railway

1940
Radnor House and St Margaret's House destroyed by enemy bomb

1965
London Borough of Richmond-upon-Thames created including Twickenham

2005
Jubilee Gardens opened

1926
Town constituted as a borough

1935
Lido opened at Riverside

2002
Museum opens

20th Century Britain

1914
First World War begins

1926
John Logie Baird obtains first television picture

1939
Outbreak of Second World War

1956
Suez Crisis

1966
England win World Cup

1969
First man on the Moon

1982
Falklands Conflict

1,000 YEARS OF HISTORY –
FROM PREHISTORY
TO THE TUDORS

A VIEW OF THE TOWN AND RIVER 1890 23537

MENTION TWICKENHAM to anyone in Britain today, and their immediate association is with the world-famous rugby stadium, venue for international rugby matches and, in recent years, rock concerts. In fact, its recorded history, as a settlement on the River Thames, dates back over 1,000 years. Over the centuries Twickenham's popularity has ebbed and flowed like the River Thames on whose banks it stands.

The 18th century was the town's golden age, when possession of a riverside house here was the height of fashion and the wealthy, famous and artistic flocked to Twickenham. It has seen many changes since then; today it is a settled, residential suburb of outer London, and has been part of the London Borough of Richmond-upon-Thames since 1965. But everywhere there are reminders of the past, a past which has been celebrated in art, music, literature and verse throughout the centuries.

Nestled in a sweeping bend of the Thames below Richmond Hill, Twickenham's sheltered riverside location first attracted prehistoric man over 4,000 years ago. In 1966, archaeologists excavating near the Thames, behind Nos 48 and 49 Church Street, found mesolithic and neolithic flints and pottery in a watercourse crossing the upper end of the car park. Other neolithic finds have been made in the riverbed near Eel Pie Island and on the island itself, which may once have been connected by a causeway to the Twickenham bank.

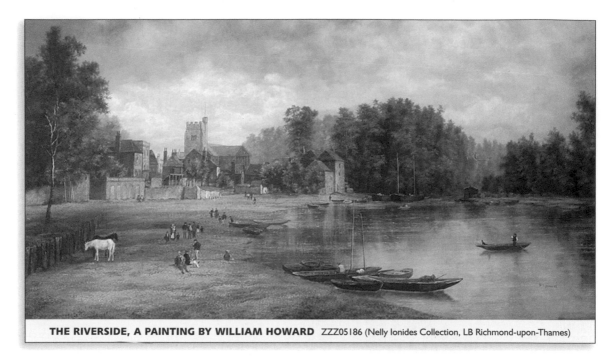

THE RIVERSIDE, A PAINTING BY WILLIAM HOWARD ZZZ05186 (Nelly Ionides Collection, LB Richmond-upon-Thames)

Evidence of Iron-Age occupation (pits, pottery and flint implements) was uncovered in 1994 at St John's Hospital in Amyand Park Road and a late Roman enclosure ditch (AD 350-400), found in the same area, may indicate the presence of a small Roman farmstead in Strafford Road near the hospital.

In 1999 a Bronze-Age ditch containing struck flints was excavated at Pope's Grotto (the public house in Cross Deep).

In the earliest records Twickenham was part of the Saxon Hundred of Hounslow and predates Richmond on the opposite bank of the River Thames by hundreds of years. (There was no direct access between the two settlements until Richmond bridge was built in 1777.) For centuries Twickenham looked to the coach roads north of the Thames and the river itself for its communications and established early links with nearby communities in Middlesex: Isleworth, Brentford, Feltham and Whitton.

The first written mention of a settlement at Twickenham occurs in a Saxon charter of 704 when Swaefred, King of Essex, and other nobles witnessed the grant of land in Twickenham (then spelt 'Tuican hom' and 'Tuiccanham') to Bishop Waldhere of London.

The land was recorded as in 'the Province which is called Middleseaxon' and bounded by the Thames to the south and east and to the north by a flood plain called the Fishbourne (presumably the flood plain of the River Crane). In 793 we find Offa granting the same land to the Archbishop of Canterbury, and later King Edmund of Wessex restored it to Christchurch Canterbury, a grant confirmed by Edred in 948.

A PAINTING OF LADY GODIVA BY JOHN COLLIER ZZZ05187 (Author's Collection)

Fact File

In 1060 the manor of Isleworth (which included Twickenham) was held by Earl Algar from Mercia, the son of the Earl of Mercia and Lady Godiva. His sons were the Earls Edwin and Morcar, allies of King Harold who was defeated at the Battle of Hastings in 1066 by William the Conqueror. After William I conquered England in 1066, he assigned the country's manorial estates to his followers and courtiers. The Manor of Isleworth, which included Twickenham, was granted to his second cousin, Walter of St Valery.

ISLEWORTH IN THE DOMESDAY BOOK

In the Domesday survey of 1086, the manor of Isleworth (written as Gistelesworde) included: two mills, meadowland, pasture for village livestock, one and a half weirs (for fishing), and woodland for 500 pigs; the total acreage in Isleworth is estimated at around 4,350 acres (of which around 2,500 were in Twickenham and Whitton) supporting a local population of around 550.

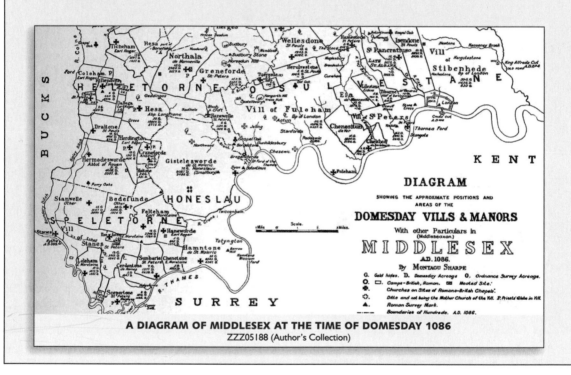

A DIAGRAM OF MIDDLESEX AT THE TIME OF DOMESDAY 1086
ZZZ05188 (Author's Collection)

The early Middle Ages after the Norman Conquest were marked by disputes between the Plantagenet kings and a powerful group of barons. In 1214, a reluctant King John was compelled by the barons to sign Magna Carta at Runnymede, recognising 'the law of the land'. The king died suddenly in 1216 and was succeeded by his nine-year-old son Henry III who, when he came of age, began to rule in the manner of his feudal ancestors. The stage was now set for a prolonged power struggle between the monarchy and the barons. It was in this troubled period (in 1227) that Henry III assigned the manor of Isleworth, including the settlement at Twickenham, to his younger brother Richard, Earl of Cornwall. As Lord of the Manor of Isleworth, the young Earl of Cornwall built himself a stone manor house (in today's old Isleworth) surrounded by a moat, and also enclosed a large area of land for a park with a double ditch and hedge. Within the park pale were fish-ponds, cattle, granaries, barns, woodland, and a rabbit warren.

Discontent with Henry's rule simmered until 1258, when it erupted into outright rebellion. The barons, led by Simon de Montfort, the King's brother-in-law, forced Henry to accept the Provisions of Oxford, expelling his favourites from England and appointing a committee of 24 to reform the government. In 1261 Henry III renounced the Provisions of Oxford and reasserted his right to appoint councillors.

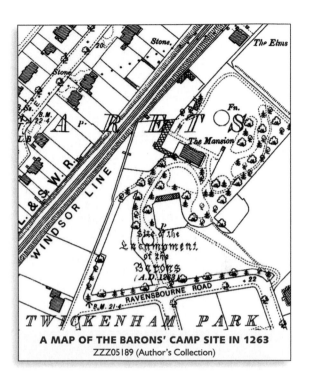

A MAP OF THE BARONS' CAMP SITE IN 1263
ZZZ05189 (Author's Collection)

Fact File

In 1263, the barons camped outside Isleworth Park to demand that Henry III implement the Provisions of Oxford. The location of their camp, in what is now Twickenham Park, is underneath Park House Gardens, but is marked on old maps. Local road names, Baronsfield Road and The Barons, also recall this connection.

In 1264, the manor house and park at Isleworth were sacked during the general uprising. Simon de Montfort led the barons to victory over the king at the Battle of Lewes in Sussex and Henry was taken prisoner. The Earl of Cornwall took refuge in a windmill where he too was captured. Although the king was not formally deposed, Simon de Montfort was de facto ruler for the next 15 months. In 1264 he proposed a new form of government, the Forma Regiminis, by which a Council of Nine would be appointed to advise the king on his choice of ministers. In 1265 he established representation by the shires in the Westminster Parliament, with two knights from every shire and two burgesses from certain nominated towns summoned - in effect an embryonic House of Commons.

However de Montfort's triumph was short-lived. The King's troops rallied under his son Prince Edward and de Montfort was captured and killed at the Battle of Evesham in August 1265, and his body was dismembered. In 1266 Henry issued the Dictum of Kenilworth restoring his authority and annulling the Provisions of Oxford. In 1272 he was succeeded by his son Edward, who went on to conquer Wales, formally annexing it to England in 1284.

Meanwhile the Earl of Cornwall continued to own the manor at Isleworth. There is a reference in his accounts for 1296-7 to Alan, vicar of Twickenham, (although the earliest recorded account of a vicar of St Mary's Parish Church in Twickenham dates from 1332). The manor house at Isleworth was rebuilt after the rebellions of the 13th century but seems to have been in poor repair by the 14th century.

Later, in 1375, a hunting lodge was built at the southern end of the park where Cassilis Road, Twickenham, is today.

In 1415 Henry V established a monastery for the Bridgettine Sisters close to the site of the modern Twickenham Bridge. It was not a success - the Sisters found the location damp and uncongenial, and soon moved upriver to Syon Park. A drainage ditch dug at the time is now an ornamental lake in the grounds of St Margaret between Ailsa Road and St George's Road. The Isleworth manor house and buildings within the moat were leased out in 1506 to John Fox, Bishop of Winchester, who held a lease of Moat Place and the adjoining derelict mill-house at Isleworth.

Isleworth Park underwent several changes of name around this time. In 1440 it became the New Park of Shene and, after 1504, it was renamed the New Park of Richmond when Henry VII renamed Shene as Richmond. The boundary between Twickenham and Isleworth manors appears to have settled around now on the ecclesiastical parish boundary which ran from the west, near today's Ivy Bridge, to join the Thames at the top of Duck's Walk. (In the 16th century it is not easy to distinguish Twickenham manorial lands from those of Isleworth, as various assets and rights associated with the two estates changed hands many times.)

By the end of the 16th century the southern end of the old Isleworth Manor was known as the Twickenham Park Estate, with a substantial house on the river facing the Royal Palace at Shene. This was Twickenham Park House, which was sited directly on the parish boundary between Twickenham and Isleworth, and even had an iron cross in the hall marking the boundary of the two parishes.

Gordon House, today located in the grounds of the former Maria Grey College, stands on the site of the original Twickenham Park park-keeper's house in 1437; it has a long and complex architectural history, and contains a 'flying' staircase by Nicholas Dubois, and a wing by Robert Adam dating from 1758.

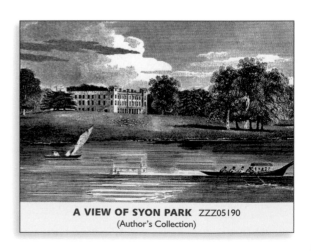

A VIEW OF SYON PARK ZZZ05190
(Author's Collection)

GORDON HOUSE AND ITS BOUNDARY WALL 2005 T91701k (Hazelle Jackson)

SIR FRANCIS BACON

Sir Francis Bacon, Lord Chancellor of England from 1618-1620, lived at Twickenham Park from 1580-1608, and loved the area. Financial pressures obliged him to sell in 1608, which he bitterly regretted. When he became Lord Chancellor, he endeavoured to buy the estate back without success: 'Let Twitnam Parke, which I sold in my younger years, be purchased, if possible, for a residence for such deserving persons to study in, since I experimentally found the situation of that place much convenient for the trial of philosophical conclusions.'

SIR FRANCIS BACON (1561-1626)
ZZZ05192 (Author's Collection)

Mills were essential to life in medieval England. They were used to grind corn and oil, and produce many of the essentials of life at the time. Many of the mills recorded in the 1086 Domesday Book incorporated eel traps to supplement diets and incomes.

Locally, the River Crane has provided water-power to mills for many centuries; its source is in the high ground between Pinner and Harrow where a series of small brooks join to form a larger stream called Yeading Brook. At Cranford Park the stream becomes a river, the River Crane. South of Cranford, the Crane forms the boundaries of Heston and Isleworth, and this was the boundary of Isleworth Manor by 1299.

In 1370, there are records of two water-mills locally, one on the Crane, the other on a stream called the Bourne (later Burkett's Brook) which ran through Whitton to join the Crane near St Margaret's; part of its course dried up after the Duke's River was built. The mill at Isleworth was rented to Bishop Fox in the 16th century. As it belonged to Syon Abbey he granted the Abbey a new mill in exchange. The new mill was between Twickenham and Isleworth, probably on the River Crane.

A medieval water mill on the Crane at Oldford near Hanworth Bridge disappeared between 1340 and 1351. There are also records of a windmill on the edge of the heath, just east of the current junction between Percy Road and Hospital Bridge Road. This disappeared between 1675 and 1743.

AN OLD MIDDLESEX WATER MILL ZZZ05193 (Author's Collection)

The Earl of Cornwall built stew (fish) ponds on the western boundary of his estate, and fish was an important part of the medieval diet. Fish weirs were used to trap fish in rivers, and were an important and often hotly disputed resource up to the 18th century. They were supposed to be licensed, but illegal weirs flourished and were a hazard to river traffic. There was at least one weir in the river by Isleworth with stakes at its upper end, and this gave its name to the modern Railshead Road where the Crane joins the Thames.

In the Middle Ages the settlement at Twickenham was a cluster of houses in streets around St Mary's Church and in narrow alleys nearby leading down to the river. Church Street was the principal way through Twickenham for travellers until the end of the 19th century when the present York Street was built. The name of Burgate was used for the area near the church in

THE RIVER CRANE JOINS THE RIVER THAMES AT RAILSHEAD ROAD 2005 ZZZ05194 (Hazelle Jackson)

1486. Although the nave of the present St Mary's dates from 1713, when it was rebuilt after it collapsed, the ragstone church tower is medieval and may have formed part of an earlier fortification on the site.

Fact File

Henry VI's cook and his wife are buried in St Mary's churchyard, Twickenham. Their memorial in the church (translated from the Latin) says, 'Here lies Richard Burton Esquire lately principal cook to his Majesty the King (Henry VI) and Agnes his Wife who died the 24th day of July 1443 of whom may God have mercy on their souls.'

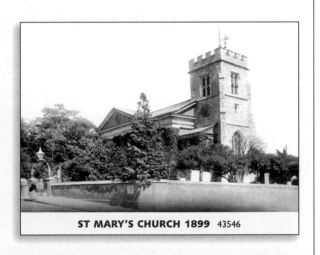

ST MARY'S CHURCH 1899 43546

The local population in the Middle Ages made a living from agriculture, fishing, boat-building, and ferrying traffic up and down the river. There was even a local vineyard, which produced 'two tuns and one pipe' in 1297. This seems to have been planted with cherry-trees later. There is little detailed evidence on the number of people living at Twickenham during the Middle Ages but the manor of Isleworth, including Twickenham, seems to have expanded slowly during this period. In the 14th century there are accounts of crops of oats, wheat, and barley being grown locally, and local livestock included cows and sheep. The rolls also list a ploughman, a shepherd, a cowman, and a dairymaid in this period. By 1547 the people of Isleworth were said to number 400, and the figure relating to Twickenham apart from the rest of Isleworth Manor is estimated at 210.

The River Thames has been an important means of transport since before the Romans arrived in England. As there was no bridge across the Thames from Twickenham on the Middlesex bank over to the Surrey bank until the 18th century, residents who wanted to cross to the opposite bank of the river did so by ferry. The first evidence of a ferry at Twickenham occurs in 1443.

A VIEW OF THE RIVER 1899 43058

THE FERRY ZZZ05195 (Hazelle Jackson Collection)

An ancient track is said to have led 'from Church Street up to the north bank of the river Thames, where there was a ferry to Richmond'. The track crossed the Great East Field, then 'open' with its 'shots', riverside pastures, and a rabbit warren, and passed along the boundary of Twickenham Park. The River Thames was also used as a thoroughfare by barges carrying goods and people. In 1534 Henry VIII passed Twickenham by river with Anne Boleyn on his way from Hampton Court to Greenwich.

Although Twickenham was primarily agricultural at this time, there was one industrial process carried out locally - the manufacture of gunpowder - which took place on the banks of the River Crane to the north-west of the town for over 400 years.

AN EARLY FLINTLOCK ZZZ05196 (Hazelle Jackson)

21

**THE TOWER AT CRANE PARK UNDERGOING
RESTORATION 1990** T91702k (Hazelle Jackson)

THE RESTORED CRANE PARK TOWER 2005
ZZZ05271 (Hazelle Jackson)

GUNPOWDER

Gunpowder, which was invented during the first half of the 14th century, is a mixture of potassium nitrate (saltpetre), charcoal, and sulphur in a ratio of 75:15:10. It was used in guns, time-fuses, and fireworks. Until the reign of Henry VIII, the lack of saltpetre in England meant most gunpowder was imported. However, as British naval power expanded beyond Europe during the reign of Elizabeth I it became possible to manufacture gunpowder at home, and by the middle of the 16th century gunpowder mills had been established at Hounslow Heath on the River Crane. One of the constituents of gunpowder is charcoal. This was produced from willow and alder, which was readily available from the river banks. The river also provided water-power for the mills and transport for barges. The open land, relatively distant from settlements, was an added advantage as gunpowder manufacture is highly dangerous.

The medieval park of Isleworth Manor lay just inside Twickenham Parish, and became detached from the manorial estate in 1506 around the time Twickenham Park House was built.

The Victoria County History of England records that 'the estate which in the 15th century was sometimes called the manors of Twickenham, Worton and Whitton, later became known as Twickenham, York's or York Hold .... it consisted of lands originally held both of Isleworth manor and of the rectory. Its lords held courts in the 15th century, and in 1650 it had 13 free tenants and 36 copyholders.'

The first explicit references to the Twickenham Manor Estate occur in 1445-6, when it is recorded that the estate belonged to William York (or Yorke); at this time, it included 80 acres of land, meadow 'sufficient for 3 virgates', and a fishery at Petersham Weir. York(e) Farm held land in central Twickenham as well as in the common fields in Twickenham, Whitton and Isleworth. The land around York House in Twickenham today was originally the site of York(e) farm, which belonged to the York family in the 15th and 16th centuries.

The York family were substantial landowners locally by the 16th century and probably lived in Twickenham Manor House, later called Arragon House and then Arragon Tower. This is thought to have been built in the 15th century and stood diagonally opposite St Mary's Church. Its park extended nearly as far north as today's Amyand Park Road, next to the railway line. Among the York family holdings locally were a mill-house with querns and the lease of the Earl of Cornwall's rabbit warren in Isleworth. The Twickenham Manor Estate passed down by

YORK HOUSE 1899 43543

inheritance to Thomas York, who preferred to live in Ramsbury in Wiltshire where the family also held land, and he sold his Twickenham property in 1538 to Edward Seymour, Earl of Hertford - the later Duke of Somerset and Lord Protector. In 1541 Hertford exchanged it with the crown for lands elsewhere. Queen Elizabeth and Edward VI granted Yorke Farm to members of their households. Queen's Farm, which also formed part of the royal estates locally, is believed to have been on or near the site of the later Orleans House. In the 17th century, Charles I gave Twickenham Manor to his Queen, Henrietta Maria. It was sold during the Protectorate, but after the Restoration the Queen Mother resumed possession of it. In 1670 it was settled for life on Catherine of Braganza, Charles II's Queen.

A POSTCARD OF A RABBIT HUNT ZZZ05197 (Hazelle Jackson Collection)

Fact File

Rabbits were an important part of the medieval economy. They were bred under licence, in closely guarded warrens, and were a much-prized commodity for providing food and fur. The Earl of Cornwall's warren was one of several local warrens originally established in the area where the sandy soil near the riverbanks was ideal terrain. Rabbits were reared by warreners in pillow mounds (warrens named after their shape) along the River Crane and near the banks of the Thames. In 1513 the Venetian envoy to the court in England reported: 'In England it is always windy and however warm the natives invariably wear furs.'

SECRET SOCIETIES AND SECRET PASSAGES

In 'Priest Holes and Hiding Places', by Allan Fea (1908), there is an intriguing reference to a secret passage leading from Arragon Tower - the name then used for the surviving portion of the former Twickenham Manor House which formerly stood on the eastern end of Church Street near St Mary's Church:

'The entrance is in the top room of the one remaining turret by means of a movable panel in the wall opposite the window. The panel displaced, you see the top of a thick wall (almost on a line with the floor of the room).

The width of the aperture is, I should think, nearly three feet; that of the wall-top about a foot and a half; the remaining space between the wall-top and the outer wall of the house is what you might perhaps term 'a chasm' - it is a sheer drop to the cellars of the house. I was told by the workmen that by walking the length of the wall-top (some fifteen feet), I should reach a stairway conducting to the vaults below, and that on reaching the bottom, a passage led off in the direction of the river, the tradition being that it actually went beneath the river to Ham House.'

Arragon Tower, the last remaining portion of Twickenham Manor House, was demolished in 1934. According to a contemporary report, Tudor bricks were recovered and sent to Hampton Court Palace; and coins were found, one dated 1240.

The Civil War (1642-6) was a time when no-one could be sure who was their enemy and who their friend, and secret groups and societies abounded. Ham House on the Surrey bank of the River Thames was built in the early 17th century, and was the scene of much political activity during the Civil War when it was owned by the Countess of Dysart, Duchess of Lauderdale, a founder member of the Society of the Sealed Knot. Today it is owned by the National Trust.

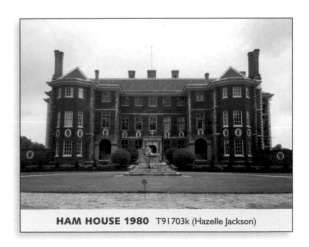

HAM HOUSE 1980 T91703k (Hazelle Jackson)

CHAPTER TWO

'AN ABUNDANCE OF CURIOUS SEATS' – TWICKENHAM 1600-1800

THE QUEEN'S HEAD INN ON THE RIVERSIDE 1890 23536A

THE 17TH CENTURY started in Twickenham with an outbreak of bubonic plague that reached the town from London in 1605 when 67 deaths were recorded in the church's burial register. Other outbreaks followed, and a Pest House ('pest' being short for pestilence) was established on the far side of Twickenham Green in the early 1600s.

In 1665 a further 24 deaths were recorded in Twickenham. There were intermittent outbreaks of plague throughout the 15th, 16th and 17th centuries before the disease died out in Europe, although there continued to be major epidemics in India and the Far East long after this. (In recent years the plague has re-emerged with sporadic outbreaks in New Mexico, USA.)

BUBONIC PLAGUE

Bubonic plague is a contagious bacterial disease characterised by fever, delirium and the formation of swollen inflamed lymph glands, called buboes. It is usually transmitted by the bites of fleas from infected rodents. The bacteria infect the bloodstream (causing septicaemic plague) and/or the lungs (pneumonic plague). In septicaemic plague there is bleeding into the skin; this creates black patches on the skin that gave it the name Black Death. Pneumonic plague is spread by droplets expelled into the air. Both forms are fatal but can be treated today by antibiotics.

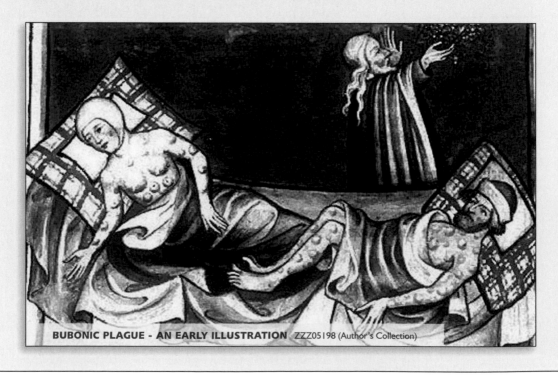

BUBONIC PLAGUE - AN EARLY ILLUSTRATION ZZZ05198 (Author's Collection)

The original manor house at Isleworth seems to have survived into the 14th century and Moses Glover's map of 1635 ascribes the house to 'Ofley kt.' In 1643, Sir John Offlcy received a lease from the Earl of Northumberland of the Moat House in Isleworth. He rebuilt the house, which was leased again in 1661. Later, a house on the same site or nearby, called Somerset House, was said to have been occupied by the widow of Charles, Duke of Somerset. It was finally pulled down in 1803, and by 1851 the only evidence of its existence was the small arm of the Duke's River east of Percy Gardens which seemed to represent the west side of its moat.

Sir Francis Bacon, who was living at Twickenham Park House in the early 17th century, sold the estate to Lucy Harrington, Countess of Bedford (1581-1627) in 1608. The Countess was a noted gardener who seems to have rebuilt the house (there are reports of a new house on the site in 1609), and also created there one of the earliest and most celebrated Renaissance gardens in England at the time.

Fact File

The first weeping willow in England is said to have been grown at Twickenham Park at the beginning of the 18th century. Another early specimen was a feature of Alexander Pope's garden on the other side of Twickenham.

AN OLD PRINT OF TWICKENHAM PARK ZZZ05191 (Author's Collection)

In 1635 the town archery butts stood at the eastern entrance to Twickenham in Richmond Road - a reminder of the need for a standing army in a constant state of readiness for war abroad. However, in the 17th century the citizens of England found themselves engaged in a different and more sinister war, the English Civil War which lasted from 1642-6. This pitted Protestants against Catholics, Parliamentarians against Royalists. It was followed by the Commonwealth and Protectorate under Cromwell, and the restoration of the Stuart monarchy under Charles II in 1660.

At different times in the turmoil which gripped the country during these years both Protestants and Roman Catholics were persecuted, and many prominent figures retired from life in town to manage their estates in the safer countryside. This, together with ideas from the Renaissance which were reaching England, promoted the growing interest in garden design which was to reach its height in the 18th century.

In 1636 the York(e) farm estate was held by Andrew Pitcarne, a groom of the King's Chamber. Moses Glover's map of 1635 shows a building in the vicinity of today's York House, covered in scaffolding and surrounded by a number of smaller structures, some of which line the roads. This is marked 'Mr Pecarne's house', and most authorities regard it as marking the construction of the current York House. The central portion of York House dates from 1635, and is one of the oldest surviving buildings locally.

YORK HOUSE FROM THE BRIDGE c1955 T91015

It was a well-equipped house. The Parliamentary Survey of June 1650 gives the following description of the property: '…all that capital messuage called Yorkes farms in Twikenham houses, buildings, structures, granaries, stables, dovecots, gardens, orchards, flower gardens, lands, meadows, pastures… hereditaments of all sorts…'

In 1656 the Pitcarne family sold York House to the Earl of Manchester - who appears to have supported both sides at different times during the Civil War and the Restoration - although they retained the nearby house, later named Orleans House. In 1661 the Earl of Manchester sold York House to the Earl of Clarendon, and it passed, with the manorial rights, to his second son, the Earl of Rochester, who is mentioned as being at Twickenham in the 1680s.

The remaining Crown holding in the area in 1669 was the Queen's Farm. From the mid 16th century this appears to have included a house on the river to the east of the town centre with 53 acres of land. Like the other Crown property, it was leased to royal officials. During the 17th century, the Pitcarne family also acquired the Queen's Farm Estate but sold it to Richard Webb in c1660, the year of the Restoration. Webb built a house there which was occupied in 1694 by Jane Davies, who lent it to Queen Anne. The Duke of Gloucester exercised his regiment of boys on the ait (small island) there, since joined to the mainland.

Directly on the river opposite the centre of Twickenham lies Eel Pie Island, one of several aits formed on bends in the river along this stretch. Originally called Twickenham Ait (and in 1604 Parish Ayte) it was a popular venue for outings as early as the 17th century, possibly earlier. Moses Glover's map of 1635 notes a plot of land on the island marked as a 'A Boulding Alley' which may have been an early bowling alley. It was reached by ferry until a footbridge was constructed in the 1950s.

THE FERRY IN MIDSTREAM 1899 43057

In 1650, the grounds of Twickenham manor house were said to be 'plentifully planted with curious and various sorts of fruit trees, roots, plants, and flowers', and the locality was also noted for its market gardens and nurseries. The growing population of the town is also evidenced by the foundation of St Mary's School in 1645. As Twickenham grew in popularity during the 17th century, so smart houses and gardens proliferated along the waterfront, in the town and out towards its edge, on the green.

Houses built at this time included:

• Lebanon Park on the riverside (later renamed Mount Lebanon), which was built by Sir James Pemberton (1545-1613), Lord Mayor of London from 1611-12. G R Holmes, a Twickenham builder, later rebuilt it in 1794 with 41 rooms.

• York House in Richmond Road, now the council offices of the London Borough of Richmond-upon-Thames. This was rebuilt around the original farm on the site in 1635 by Andrew Pitcarne. It was bought by the local council in the early 20th century.

• The Copt Hall estate, behind Heath Road where Holly Road now is. It was admired for its 'hanging gardens' which reached as far as the River Crane in the 18th century. The estate was purchased in the 1840s by local developer Sir Charles Freake, and the remaining property was demolished soon afterwards. The name remains in the present Copthall Gardens.

• Richmond House on the south side of King Street, with extensive grounds, which was originally built in the 17th century. It was replaced later in 1816, but in 1923 was purchased and pulled down by Twickenham UDC to widen the road. Municipal swimming baths were erected on the site in 1935.

• Radnor House, one of the largest houses in the town, which was built in 1672-3 on the banks of the Thames at Cross Deep. From

RADNOR HOUSE ZZZ05199
(LB Richmond-upon-Thames Local Studies Collection)

1722 it was the home of the Earl of Radnor. Like Pope's Villa nearby it had extensive gardens on either side of the road connected by an underground passage. Extended and remodelled in the Italian style in the mid 19th century, it was purchased by Twickenham UDC in 1902 to be the council offices.

The Civil War and its aftermath caused great hardship to many working people, and local benefactors and philanthropists were moved to make provision for the needy of the parish. In 1666 and 1667 the annual poor rate was £55. In 1673 an assessment at 8d in the pound brought in £78. However, the management of these funds was badly muddled with little or no record-keeping, and the parish was constantly in trouble with the Poor Law commissioners as a result. After the Dissolution of the Monasteries in the reign of Henry VIII there was no residual body left to take over the church's role in providing social assistance and civil administration. From the 1500s this was partly remedied by Acts of Parliament requiring parishes to set up vestries to administer their affairs, and gradually these took over from manorial courts. In Twickenham the parish twice refused to form a select vestry.

A vestry was ordained by the bishop in 1674 after a petition by 'several principal inhabitants' that parish affairs were neglected and in disorder.

Out of the funds available to be administered by the vestry, poor persons - most of whom were widows - received pensions of one shilling. a week. The vestry also passed an order at this time against excessive bell-ringing, which had long been a cause of trouble, and was again the subject of an order in 1711.

In the 17th century there was a close link in the minds of the authorities between poverty and vagrancy, with vagrants generally treated as the undeserving poor. Bad behaviour by vagrants led to a spell in the stocks or a night in the town lock-up. On 1 February 1684 the Vestry ordered that the town's 'crosshouse' was to be 'made in ye manner of a cage with a strong lock and keye, and also the Stocks be repayred and a whipping post to be new set up' within a fortnight. This Crosshouse was erected in the centre of Twickenham - its owner charged to 'ward within and about this parish and to keep all Beggars and Vagabonds that shall lye abide or lurk about the Towne and to give correction to such.'

Several almshouses were built on the edge of the town in the 18th century and in 1725 the parish built a workhouse near the edge of Twickenham Green. Expenditure on the poor stood at £830 in 1775-6 and had risen rose to over £3,000 in 1814-15, with 91 adults in the workhouse, and 112 on permanent relief. In 1764 the house of correction, roundhouse, or cage was moved, with the stocks, from the middle of the town to the common, near the gate.

THE STOCKS ZZZ05200 (Author's Collection)

TWICKENHAM GREEN

In 1725 a workhouse was opened on the north side of Twickenham Green. Twickenham Green is a surviving fragment of the eastern section of Hounslow Heath, previously referred to as Twickenham Common or Little Common. This was where the Heath started, and the apex of the triangle may have been marked by a gate to the town.

TWICKENHAM GREEN 1923 ZZZ05201 (Hazelle Jackson Collection)

Not all the residents of the almshouses were as sober and well-behaved as their benefactors hoped. The records state that private distilling of gin in the adjoining almshouses disturbed the order of the workhouse in 1735.

Despite the hardships of the working classes, the popularity of Twickenham continued with the wealthier members of society and by the early 18th century Twickenham was 'a village remarkable for an abundance of curious seats'. The town's popularity at this time owed a great deal to its picturesque setting below Richmond Hill, a location which was widely admired, and was compared to the Arcadian landscapes viewed by 18th aristocrats in Italy on the Grand Tour. (Arcadia is a region of Greece symbolised from early times as an idyllic pastoral landscape that has inspired poets, artists and landscape designers.)

Marble Hill House was built on the Thames facing Ham House in 1724 for Henrietta Howard, the Countess of Suffolk and mistress of the Prince of Wales, later King George I. Its elegant neo-classical style is typical of the fashionable houses popular along the river at this period. Later in the century in 1795-6 it was briefly occupied by another royal mistress, Mrs Maria Fitzherbert (1756-1837), the morganatic wife of the Prince Regent, later George IV.

ALEXANDER POPE (1688-1744)

POPE'S BUST IN THE TEMPLE OF ENGLISH WORTHIES AT STOWE 2005
S607701k (Hazelle Jackson)

'Twit'nam, the Muses' fav'rite seat,
Twit'nam, the Graces' lov'd retreat.'

One of the most famous occupants of Twickenham was the poet and gardener, Alexander Pope, who built a famous garden and grotto on the River Thames to the west of the town in the 18th century. He was born in London on 21 May 1688, the only child of elderly, well-off, Roman Catholic parents. The family had to move out of the City of London after the 1688 Act of Parliament, which prohibited Catholics from living within 10 miles of the City of London. During his childhood Pope developed a tubercular infection of the bone that became known later as Pott's disease, and which reduced him to a hunchback - he never grew above four feet six inches. It finally left him a cripple, afflicted by constant headaches, who had to wear stays in order to stand.

From 1714-1720 Pope translated Homer's 'Iliad'. He published it to critical acclaim that established his reputation as the leading English poet of his generation. He clearly inherited some of his father's business acumen as the sale of the translation by public subscription made him financially independent from the usual political patronage of the time, which made him very proud: 'But

HOUSES ON TWICKENHAM WATERFRONT 1770 ZZZ05202 (Author's Collection)

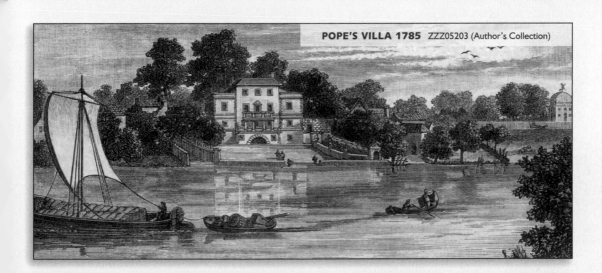

POPE'S VILLA 1785 ZZZ05203 (Author's Collection)

(thanks to Homer) since I live and thrive, Indebted to no Prince or Peer alive.' After his father's death in 1717, he and his mother moved from their home in Berkshire to a small villa with five acres of garden at Twickenham. The last 25 years of his life until 1744 were spent at 'Twitnam' as he fondly called it, where he nurtured and developed the house and garden that drew admirers from far and wide, and entertained a wide circle of friends.

Pope's garden at Twickenham became a centre of pilgrimage for his admirers. The house and grounds were later purchased by Baroness Howe, who became so exasperated with sightseers that she had the house pulled down in 1808. Pope's house and garden (on the other side of the road) are now long gone. In 2005 the original site of Pope's villa was occupied by St James Boys' School. The grotto tunnel under the road has partly survived, and is open occasionally open to the public.

Near Pope's Villa was Strawberry Hill, Horace Walpole's Gothick fantasy. Walpole extended and transformed the small house after he bought it in 1747, and assembled a great many period fittings and fixtures in keeping with his desire to return to the Gothic period. The house was later extended by Lady Frances Waldegrave, and is today part of St Mary's College.

In the 18th century wealthy men and women who wanted to make a statement, and had the funds to do so, built an extravagant house and garden. James Johnston, Secretary of State for Scotland, obtained the lease of the Queen's Farm estate in 1702, and at once commissioned a splendid new house from John James, one of Sir Christopher Wren's chief assistants. The house was erected in 1710, and has been described as 'a typical Wren

STRAWBERRY HILL ZZZ05204 (Author's Collection)

house with a mansard roof and brick walls, a Portland stone central feature and James's customary masculine and simple detailing.' This was to be called Orleans House, and overlooked the Thames near York House.

ORLEANS HOUSE ZZZ05205 (LB Richmond-upon-Thames Local Studies Collection)

In 1720 James Gibbs added the Octagon room, which is the only surviving part of the house today. Johnston remodelled the gardens which were particularly celebrated, and included canals, a mount, an icehouse, a vineyard, a parterre, a wilderness, a pleasure garden, a kitchen garden, a fruit garden, extensive vineyards and a grotto. There were also cherry trees, which seem to have been a local speciality.

Johnston lived very well; as Lady Wentworth, his neighbour, wrote at the time, ' he had a vast deal of company dayly, thear is hardly a day that he has not a coach and six horsis at his doar, and some timse twoe or three more.

Sure he must have a vast esteat to entertain soe many, and he has an abondence of men at work in the grownd before his hous …'

Mount Lebanon and Riverside House were also built in the early 18th century near Orleans House and may be on the site of former farmhouses in the area. Indeed, such was the demand for houses in 18th-century Twickenham that the first Georgian-style terraced town houses now appeared, in Montpelier Row and Sion Row in the 1720s. These delightful terraces have survived to the present day, while the old houses in large grounds have nearly all been swallowed up by later developments.

SION ROW 2005 ZZZ05256 (Hazelle Jackson)

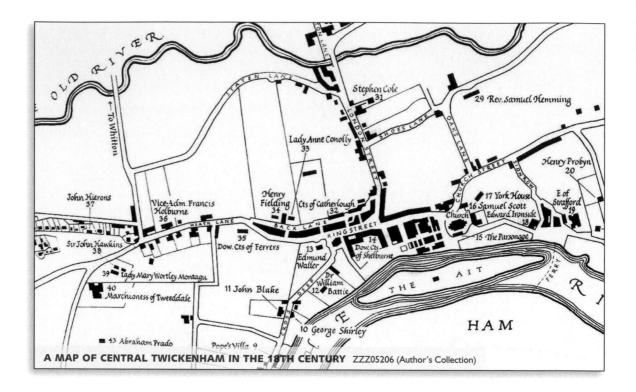

A MAP OF CENTRAL TWICKENHAM IN THE 18TH CENTURY ZZZ05206 (Author's Collection)

The town at this time provided an escape not only for non-Protestants fearing religious persecution but also for disreputable types fleeing their creditors in London. In 1722 the infamous rake Philip, Duke of Wharton took a lease on the Grove at the junction of Cross Deep and Heath Road, where the Odeon cinema used to stand and the Billiard Hall is today.

POULETT LODGE ON CROSS DEEP ZZZ05207 (Hazelle Jackson Collection)

Fact File

The nave of St Mary's Church fell down in 1713 and was rebuilt in Georgian style separately from its medieval tower. In 1713 the nave of St Mary's Church collapsed, a fact that may have been related to the structural alterations made in 1640 by the parishioners to provide more seating and better lighting. The old building was in such a poor state of structural repair that the new vicar, Dr Pratt, had refused to conduct any more services within it; emergency repairs were being discussed only three days before it collapsed. The nave was rebuilt to a design by John James, who was responsible for the Wren house built for local resident, James Johnston, in 1710. He retained the church's medieval tower, which gives it today's distinctive appearance.

ST MARY'S CHURCH c1955 T91009

THE INTERIOR OF ST MARY'S CHURCH 1899 43547

At the age of eighteen, Wharton was the youngest non-royal Duke ever created; he inherited great influence and wealth both of which he rapidly dissipated. In 1722, probably already nearly bankrupt, he arrived in Twickenham with a large entourage and, despite their common dislike of Prime Minister Walpole, enraged Alexander Pope by paying passionate suite to Lady Mary Wortley Montagu, who lived nearby. In 1725 Wharton, who was a founder member of the Hell Fire Club, left England and drifted around the continent before fleeing to Spain to avoid his creditors, where he died in 1731 at the age of 32.

In the 1740s, the activities of the habituees of a moored vessel lying near Orleans House, called The Folly, caused local residents to write to the Lord Mayor of London complaining that '…there is lately fixed near the Shore a flatbottom boat for carrying heavy loads (especially on canals) called the Folly wherein divers loose and disorderly persons are frequently entertained who have behaved in a very indecent Manner and do frequently afront persons of Fashion and desired so great a Nuisance might be removed …'.

The more sophisticated and cultured residents of the town appreciated the performing arts and, in the 1750s, Richmond Theatre summer company performed regularly in the town. The local theatre is believed to have been on the south side of King Street. It was replaced in 1877 by the new town hall.

Although primarily residential, the town was not solely devoted to pleasure.

Fact File

The young Duke of Wharton, who lived in Twickenham in 1723, formed a local chapter of the Hell Fire Club called the Schemers, ostensibly dedicated to amorous rather than blasphemous pursuits. Another 18th-century local resident associated with the Hell Fire Club was Paul Whitehead, secretary and former steward of Sir Francis Dashwood's Hell Fire club in West Wycombe.

Farming and gardening, particularly market gardening, became thriving local industries during the 18th century, supported by the demand for fruit and vegetables from the population of London. Local resident and historian Edward Ironside writing between 1780 and 1797 noted that raspberries and strawberries were sent to the London markets, and that early peas were grown in quantity. River transport remained an important means of moving goods to London, and the barges regularly travelled up and down the River Thames from Twickenham Wharf.

In the 17th century, Bishop Corbet's house stood beside the River Crane on the London Road. He was followed by local brewer Thomas Cole who built a brewery near today's railway station and later moved it across the London road to the site of the present Sorting Office. The family built Heatham House on the site of Bishop Corbet's former house, as their family home. Heatham House is today a listed building.

HEATHAM HOUSE 2005 ZZZ05623 (Hazelle Jackson)

Mills continued to flourish along the banks of the River Crane on the outskirts of the town, using water-power to create products like oil and gunpowder. Gunpowder manufacture was big business in the 17th century and James I (1602-25) granted a Royal Charter to the gunpowder manufacturers on the Heath. Crane Park Powder Mills were established between 1766 and 1768. The first mill started life as a corn mill. The gunpowder mill east of Hanworth Bridge was notorious for explosions that broke windows for miles around. In 1772 three mills blew up, shattering glass and buildings in the neighbourhood. Horace Walpole wrote complaining to his friend and relative Seymour Conway, then Lieutenant

General of the Ordnance, that all the decorative painted glass had been blown out of his windows at Strawberry Hill.

A GRAVESTONE IN CRANFORD CEMETERY OF A VICTIM OF AN ACCIDENT AT THE GUNPOWDER MILLS, PHOTOGRAPHED IN 2003
ZZZ05208 (Hazelle Jackson)

Curtis & Harvey leased the mills in 1820, and bought them outright from the Duke of Northumberland in 1871. In 1927 the licence to manufacture gunpowder was cancelled. The site was bought by a local man, Frank Yates, who tried to sell the mills as a going concern. However, the arrival of the railway had increased the local population enough to make it an unsuitable site for such a notoriously dangerous industry. Eventually he sold part of the site for housing and part to Twickenham Council, who turned it into a park. In 1990 Crane Park was made a Statutory Local Nature Reserve. Today only the restored shot-tower in the Crane valley survives as a reminder of the river's explosive past.

Twickenham's popularity made it a hub for stage-coaches. A Turnpike Act was passed in 1767 designating the road from Isleworth as a turnpike which meant that tolls could be charged for its maintenance. Initially there were problems with flooding at Cross Deep where it met Waldegrave Road; this was caused by a stream joining the Thames here, but the problem was solved by putting the stream in a culvert. The Trust continued until 1827, when all the turnpikes north of the Thames were taken over by the Commissioners of Metropolitan Turnpike Roads.

Communication with the capital was by hourly coaches and omnibuses from the King's Head and the George on King Street; these two inns were the main coaching inns in the

THE TOLL GATE AND TOLL HOUSE ON THE TURNPIKE ZZZ05209 (Author's Collection)

town and had extensive stables. The George has survived to the present day although it was remodelled internally in the 1970s, when it lost its original interior. The Crown on the Richmond Road also dates from this period.

The popularity of the area made it necessary to build a bridge over the Thames linking the road between Richmond and Twickenham, and Richmond Bridge opened in 1777. It is the oldest Thames bridge still in use. Finance for it was raised by the issue of tontine shares - when a holder died, his share was split among the remaining share-holders until all the shares fell into the hands of the last survivor. There were

two tontines: the nominee of the first died aged 86 in 1859, the survivor of the second, aged 91, in 1865. The bridge was widened between 1937-39, with great care taken to retain its original appearance.

Twickenham Park changed hands several times in the 18th century, and at the end of the century was owned by Lord Frederick Cavendish. According to one writer in 1797, the house was still substantially Elizabethan though one front had been rebuilt, and most of the rooms were very small. After Lord Cavendish's death in 1805, Twickenham Park and grounds were sold for development, and the house was demolished soon after this.

RICHMOND BRIDGE ZZZ05210 (Hazelle Jackson Collection)

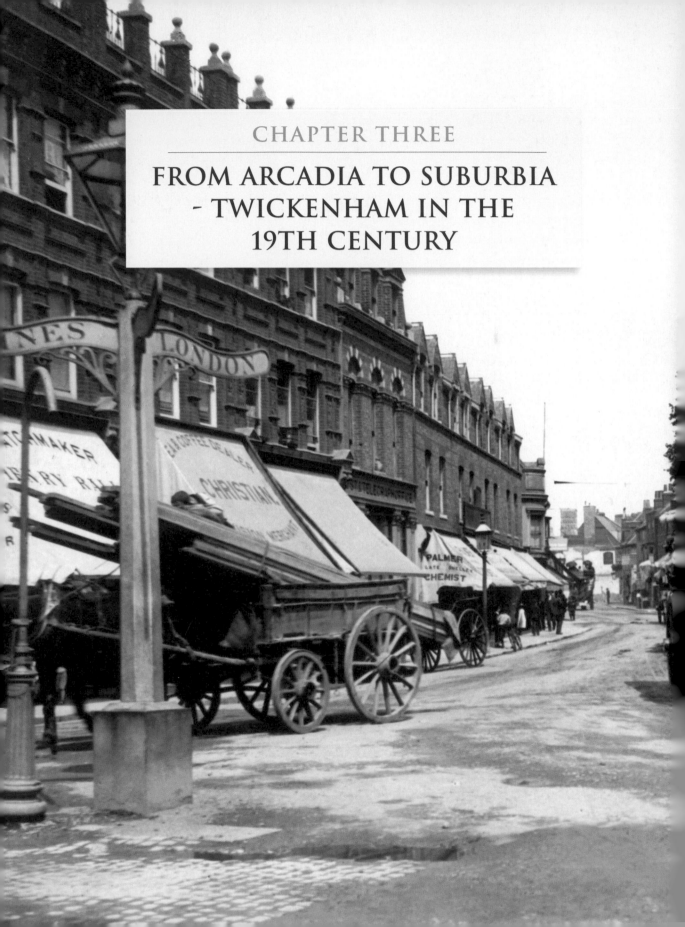

CHAPTER THREE

FROM ARCADIA TO SUBURBIA - TWICKENHAM IN THE 19TH CENTURY

KING STREET 1909 T91001

'THREE years ago, the admiral, my honoured uncle, bought a cottage at Twickenham for us all to spend our summers in; and my aunt and I went down to it quite in raptures; but it being excessively pretty, it was soon found necessary to be improved, and for three months we were all dirt and confusion, without a gravel walk to step on, or a bench fit for use. I would have every thing as complete as possible in the country, shrubberies and flower gardens, and rustic seats innumerable; but it must all be done without my care. Henry is different, he loves to be doing.' (From 'Mansfield Park' by Jane Austen, 1814.)

By the start of the 19th century the riverside, embellished with villas, was said to convey 'an idea of luxury which the utmost labours of the pen would vainly endeavour to impart'. During the Regency period the town still attracted the wealthy and the artistic with a taste for rustic cottages which now formed part of the fashionable vogue for the picturesque.

In 1801 the local population was over 3,000 and this grew fairly steadily to over 5,000 in 1841. Between 1821 and 1841 the number of houses in the parish rose from about 740 to just over 1,000, and the increasing numbers meant that a new Anglican church was needed. In 1841 Holy Trinity Church was built on Twickenham Green in 1841.

In 1812 the celebrated English artist J M W Turner, R A, designed and built a modest villa for himself and his father in East Twickenham. Sandycombe (originally Solus) Lodge has altered little since Turner's time, although the gardens, small lake and extensive views towards the Thames have long since gone. In 2004 the Friends of Turner's House group was set up to support the owner of the house, Professor Harold Livermore, in his wish to leave the house to the nation. A charitable trust was established for that purpose in 2005.

SANDYCOMBE LODGE ZZZ05211
(Author's Collection)

HOLY TRINITY CHURCH 1899 43548

In the early 19th century, the town's large houses continued to attract aristocratic owners. The town was particularly popular with the exiled French royal family; they occupied Highshot House in Crown Road (then called Crown Lane) at that time.

Fact File

The former site of Highshot House in Crown Road has an interesting history. It was occupied by members of the French Royal Family in the early 1800s. It became a Home for Inebriates in the late 1800s, and then a factory in the early 20th century. At the start of the 21st century the site was used by the St George Property Group for a new head office, in neo-Georgian style.

ST GEORGE'S HOUSE, CROWN ROAD 2005 T91706k (Hazelle Jackson)

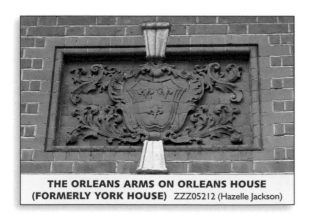

THE ORLEANS ARMS ON ORLEANS HOUSE (FORMERLY YORK HOUSE) ZZZ05212 (Hazelle Jackson)

Louis-Philippe, Duc d'Orleans (1773-1850) leased James Johnston's house (now renamed Orleans House in his honour) from 1815-17. Henri d'Orleans, Duke d'Aumale (1822-1897), lived in England for more than 23 years after the revolution of 1848. The Duc, who was the fourth son of Louis Philippe, bought York House in 1864 for his nephew, the Comte de Paris. Between 1897 and 1906 it was owned by his son, Louis Philippe Robert,

Duc d'Orleans. Other members of the family also lived in large houses in the town.

In the early 19th century London's growing population was generating increased demand for fruit and vegetables, and west Middlesex farmers and agriculturalists turned to market gardening on a large scale. This profitable use for the local land had swept away the old rabbit warrens by 1800; the only trace of them left is the reference to the Warren Footpath on old pictures of the riverside from Marble Hill to central Twickenham.

Most of the market gardens were on the north and north-east of the town between Richmond Road and Whitton Road; partly because of building round the town, they gradually spread into the former arable and mixed farmland between Whitton and the Crane. Orchards and market gardens continued to spread over the former heath land to the north and east as the century advanced.

Fact File

By 1800 there were more than nineteen inns and ale-houses in the parish, many serving the busy coaching trade. Several old inns, some dating from the 17th century, still remain, including: the George, the Fox (formerly the Bell), the Barmy Arms, (originally the Queen's Head), the Hobgoblin (formerly the Black Dog), the White Swan and the Prince Blucher.

THE FOX INN 2005 T91707k (Hazelle Jackson)

Local watermen banded together to form their own steam-packet company between 1840 and 1844, and Eel Pie Island became a popular resort for steamer excursions from London. The eel pies served there gave it its nickname, which has stuck ever since.

The novelist Charles Dickens (1812-1870) spent the summer of 1838 at No 4, Ailsa Park Villas (now No 2), and subsequently set several scenes in his novels in Twickenham including 'Nicholas Nickleby' and 'Little Doritt'.

In 'Little Dorrit', Arthur Clennam visits Mr Meagles at his cottage residence, crossing the Thames on the Twickenham ferry to Ham and back before breakfast: '... *As the morning was fine, and he had an hour on his hands, he crossed the river by the ferry, and strolled along a footpath through some meadows. When he came back to the towing path he found the ferry-boat on the opposite side, and a gentleman hailing it and waiting to be taken over.*'

A POSTCARD OF EEL-PIE-ISLAND & HOTEL
ZZZ05213 (Hazelle Jackson Collection)

In 'Nicholas Nickleby', Dickins wrote: '*It had come to pass that afternoon that Miss Morleena Kenwigs had received an invitation to repair next day, per steamer from Westminster Bridge, unto the Eel Pie Island at Twickenham, there to make merry upon a cold collation, bottled-beer, shrub and shrimps and to dance in the open air to the music of a locomotive band.*'

EELS AT TWICKENHAM

A PLATE OF STEWED EEL ZZZ05214
(From a Victorian cookery book in the author's collection)

The modern name of Eel Pie Island refers to the eels which were a popular delicacy with Londoners visiting the island on a day trip since the early 18th century. Eels have been eaten in London since medieval times when the consumption of meat was banned on religious festivals and holidays. The Thames is tidal at Twickenham (the tide turns at Teddington upstream); in April and May young eels (elvers) ascend the river from the estuary as far as Teddington but return to the sea during the winter months. Eel numbers have dropped dramatically since the 19th century.

New technology was coming to the town due to the Industrial Revolution. A night watch had first been provided by subscription in 1822, until The Lighting and Watching Act was adopted in 1833. The lighting was continued after the Metropolitan Police took over the watch duties in 1840. Gas arrived in 1858.

In 1848 the railway was constructed from Richmond to Staines, and a railway station built at Twickenham where the car and bus parks outside the former Albany Hotel are now situated. Terraced houses for railway workers were built near the station, and modest Victorian suburban villas throughout the town. The present station was built on the London Road bridge in 1954.

A highways board was formed in 1849, and a burial board under the chairmanship of the vicar in 1866. Lastly, a local board of health was formed in 1868, but it was 1876 before a satisfactory drainage and sewage scheme had been developed.

As the large houses and estates came onto the market many were snapped up by property developers. The Arragon House estate (formerly Twickenham Manor) was sold for building in 1853, including the area from Arragon House on the northern side of Church Street (opposite St Mary's Church) up as far as Amyand Park Road.

THE RAILWAY STATION 1954 ZZZ05215 (Courtesy of LB Richmond-upon-Thames, Local Studies Collection)

KING STREET 1860 ZZZ05216 (Courtesy of LB Richmond-upon-Thames Local Studies Collection)

In 1829 a new large house, Twickenham Park Mansion, was built in 1829 on the site of the former Twickenham Park House; in the early 19th century this was occupied for a time by the banker Francis Gosling. Other large houses along the waterfront in East Twickenham at this time included Gordon House and St Margaret's House.

The Earl of Cassilis, later the Marquis of Ailsa (died 1846), bought land on the boundary of the Isleworth/Twickenham parishes in the early 19th century and built a large house, St Margaret's, overlooking the Thames in the 1830s, naming his estate after it. The grounds were extended to include the part of Twickenham Park then in Isleworth parish, and Richmond Road was slightly diverted away from the house.

After his death the estate was purchased by the Earl of Kilmorey, who rebuilt St Margaret's House but never lived there. Later it was used a girls' home by the London School Board, and then became part of the Royal Naval School for Girls.

In the 1850s, the Earl of Kilmorey sold some of the land to the Conservative Land Society who developed it as the St Margaret's Trust Grounds.

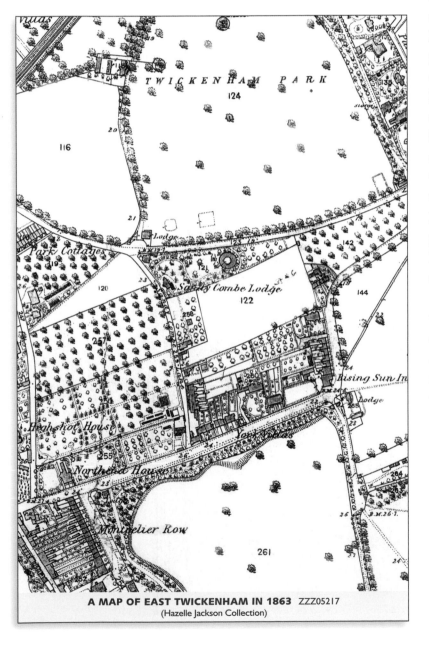

A MAP OF EAST TWICKENHAM IN 1863 ZZZ05217
(Hazelle Jackson Collection)

THE ST MARGARET'S TRUST GROUNDS

The St Margaret's Trust Grounds were laid out in 1854 by the Conservative Land Association, which drew up plans for the construction of a residential estate for gentlemen and the professional middle classes. The development was part speculation, part political gerrymandering; by building substantial properties on large plots, the Conservatives hoped to ensure the owners would qualify to vote under the Reform Act of 1832, and would vote Conservative when they did so.

About 270 properties were built around three large pleasure grounds: The Lake Grounds; The River Grounds; and The Avenue Grounds. A Trust was set up, covenants were produced to restrict the ability of owners to develop their plots, and trustees were appointed to maintain them. The original estate and its management structure remain today, and 140 properties with direct access onto the communal grounds attract a premium whenever they are put on the market.

ST MARGARET'S LODGE, HOME OF LADY MESSOM 2005 ZZZ05218 (Hazelle Jackson Collection)

Although St Margaret's Grounds are now separated from the rest of Twickenham by the Chertsey Road, the name St Margaret's had become established by 1860. St Margaret's Railway Station was opened between Richmond and Twickenham in 1876. The arrival of the railway had triggered a period of accelerated growth. The population had risen to 10,500 with over 2,000 houses in the parish by 1871. It increased again by 25% between 1891-1901.

In Twickenham around 11,000 houses were built in the 1890s and 17,000 in the next decade. Twickenham Urban District Council was formed in 1895. The population increased yet again after the arrival of trams in 1903.

RICHMOND LOCK

When the old London Bridge was demolished in 1832, the removal of the palisades constructed to protect the bridge resulted in the tides on the Thames rising and falling far more rapidly than before. Together with the dredging of the lower river, the cumulative effect was that, for long periods, the Thames at Twickenham and Richmond was little more than a stream running through mud-banks. After many years of petitioning, permission was granted in 1890 to build a half-lock and weir downstream of Richmond Bridge. This became Richmond Lock, whose ornate wrought ironwork is much admired today.

RICHMOND LOCK 2003 ZZZ05219 (Hazelle Jackson)

New forms of entertainment also arrived at the end of the century. Films started to be shown in the Town Hall, which had been built in King Street in 1877 by a private developer. Films were shown here for several years until formal cinemas were built in the town early in the 20th century. The old auditorium, which may date from the earlier theatre, was later incorporated into the Town Hall built in 1877. The Town Hall was pulled down in 1929 but the auditorium still survives behind the shops to the south of King Street. It was the subject of a planning application for conversion into flats in 2004.

Fact File

Edwardian stage beauty and royal mistress Lily Langtry made her stage debut in Twickenham in 1881. Recalling her career later she commented: 'A great many people have said that I had an early training for the stage. But I had none. I never trod the boards, even at home, till I appeared at Twickenham town hall in "A Fair Encounter".'

In the year of the Enclosure Awards (1818), First Cross Road was called Workhouse Road, and the land facing it Workhouse Allotment. This land of just over four acres occupied about half the Green as it is today. The Workhouse itself, with the adjacent almshouses stood just to the north across the road then named Hanworth, and now called Twickenham Road. The remainder of the land was allocated to the 'Twickenham

Poor', having been set aside in 1818 as part compensation for the loss of fuel rights on the common land.

The speed of development and loss of the

ST MARY'S CHURCH 1899 43059

old countryside around the town affected the local working classes and smallholders particularly badly at this time. They had few alternative sources of income, and many ended up in the slums of the alleys and narrow streets leading down to the Embankment in the late 19th century. Many of the wealthy citizens of the town took little interest in the

administration of poor relief - an attitude criticised by the Brougham Commission in 1823. However, the commissioners were unable to unravel the general confusion between parish and charity funds, because the origin of so many of the charities was doubtful, and no records existed of the purpose to which their donors intended them to be put. The parish left much of the work in the hands of its officers, which resulted in sporadic embezzlement.

In 1860 there were 22 people receiving alms, and living in poverty and discomfort. Remonstrations from the Charity Commissioners brought about a new system, but poverty and deprivation continued in the slums near the river. In 1875 the

Rev H F Limpus, vicar of Twickenham, wrote in the parish magazine about a hovel of two rooms containing a family of six with another expected, adding that 'Not one wealthy man would allow his cattle to be housed in such places as I could point out to him'. He ended with a plea for change: 'then we might sweep away for ever the block of sheds and hovels extending from the church down to Water Lane'.

To offer some relief to the local poor, a Mission Hall was built on the Embankment in 1870 on land donated by John Bowyer in 1869. In 1892 an annexe was added to serve soup and hot food for the needy during hard weather.

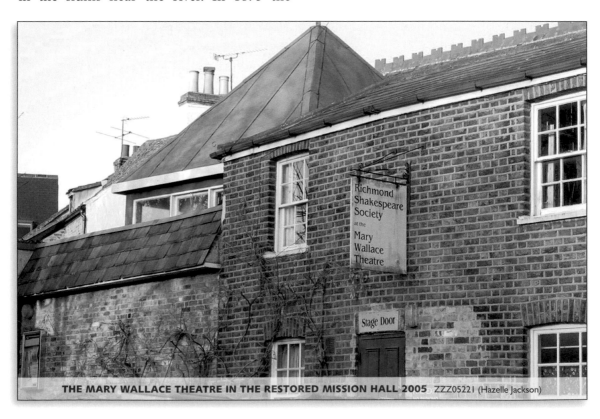

THE MARY WALLACE THEATRE IN THE RESTORED MISSION HALL 2005 ZZZ05221 (Hazelle Jackson)

ST JOHN'S HOSPITAL

ST JOHN'S HOSPITAL ZZZ05222 (Author's Collection)

In 1876 Elizabeth Twining restored the local almshouses at her own expense and in 1898 they were occupied by widows of the parish. Miss Twining also purchased Amyand Park House to the east of the London Road (the façade can still be glimpsed behind later buildings) and founded St John's Hospital in the grounds for the 'benefit of the sick and suffering in and around Twickenham'. It was opened in 1880 by H R H The Duchess of Teck, accompanied by the duke and three of their children.

The Illustrated London News reported that 'the Duchess was led through the corridor to the women's ward where a special service was conducted by the Rev G B Twining, the honorary Chaplain. Dr Benthall, the resident medical officer, and Mrs Benthall held a garden party after the ceremony and received the Royal visitors who remained some time.'

THE PLAQUE ON THE ALMSHOUSES RESTORED BY THE LIBERALITY OF ELIZABETH TWINING, TODAY ON THE WALL OF ST MARY'S CHURCH
ZZZ05260 (Hazelle Jackson)

Elizabeth Twining, the philanthropist who lived in Dial House on the riverside from 1866 until her death in 1889, left Dial House to the parish and it has been occupied as a vicarage since that time. It takes its name from the vertical sundial on the front of the house, and was the residence of the Bishop of Kensington in 2005.

The town experienced a severe spell of weather in January 1881, which froze the Thames and created up to 14-foot-deep snowdrifts. An ox was roasted on the Thames near Eel Pie Island. The print shown below, capturing the scene at Twickenham, was taken from one of a number of 'instantaneous photographs' taken by Mr J Thompson, which appeared in The Illustrated London News of 5 Feb 1881, entitled 'Scenes on the Frozen Thames'.

Development continued around the town

DIAL HOUSE, RIVERSIDE 2005 ZZZ05259
(Hazelle Jackson)

during the second half of the 19th century as the old estates came on to the market. When Lord Kilmorey's land in the old Isleworth and Twickenham Park estate came on the market after his death in 1880, it was covered with semi-detached or terraced houses closely packed in smaller streets.

THE FROZEN RIVER THAMES 1881 ZZZ05223 (from The Illustrated London News)

ROSSLYN ROAD IN ST MARGARET'S 2005 ZZZ05224
(Hazelle Jackson)

A Victorian house in Twickenham Park grounds.

Cambridge House, and its 30-acre estate, was sold for redevelopment in 1897, and is now covered by Alexander, Cresswell, Morley and Denton Roads. The houses that were built were let at £36-£52 a year. Substantial villas were also built in the area between St Margaret's Road and the Richmond Road.

York House remained in private ownership. Occupants during the 19th century included Mrs Damer, the sculptress, Sir Alexander Johnson, former chief justice of Ceylon, the Duchess of Roxburghe, the Comte de Paris, Sir Mountstuart Grant Duff, Governor of Madras, and the Duc d'Orleans.

During her long reign Queen Victoria celebrated two jubilees, a Golden Jubilee in 1887 and a Diamond Jubilee in 1897. These were occasions for much public rejoicing. Flags, bunting and decorations were hung out, commemorative glass and china souvenirs were sold, and thousands of residents turned out in their Sunday best for the meals, ceremonies, processions and celebrations to mark the occasion.

THE DIAMOND JUBILEE 1897 ZZZ05225 (Courtesy of LB Richmond-upon-Thames Local Studies Collection)

No riverside town would be complete without a rowing club, and Twickenham Rowing Club was founded in 1860. Cricket too arrived in the 19th century - the first recorded match played by Twickenham Cricket Club was on July 29th 1833 against Thames Ditton - but it was in the next century that the world famous rugby ground would be established on 'Billy Williams's cabbage patch'.

The pace of change accelerated as the 20th century approached, and after its formation in 1895 the new Urban District Council embarked on a programme of renovation. The local board had constructed the embankment between 1875 and 1882, and planned a new street, York Street, in 1892 that would bypass Church Street. This opened in 1899.

The Public Libraries Act was adopted in 1882, and the library was situated in the town hall until 1907 when it moved to the present Carnegie building in Garfield Road; this was undergoing extensive renovation in 2005.

CHARLIE SHORE'S REGATTA

Local waterman Charlie Shore founded the Boys and Girls Regatta in 1894. This was a popular event which continued until the Second World War, and concluded with a firework show and a set piece by Charlie Shore himself.

THE VIEW FROM THE ISLAND 1890 23535

In February 1898 the surveyor reported that the delays in breaking up the granite at the workhouse had delayed him in repairing the roads; he was authorised to hire a steam roller for one month. In May that year, York Street was cut through the east end of the town to bypass Church Street after Page's corner - where York Street now starts at the junction with the London Road - was knocked down.

The Richmond and Twickenham Times reported that: 'Page's Corner, one of the most dangerous in the County of Middlesex has disappeared. For many years past the business of draper was carried on by Mr Page, a very old resident who although somewhat eccentric in manner and dress was deservedly respected by residents.'

Local working-class residents were still expected to know their place and behave themselves. When a fair came to Twickenham Green in 1898, the medical officer reported to the council that: 'For several days past this land has been occupied for a fair. There is a large steam switchback, swings, coconut and dummy shies, and trials of strength in which mallets are used. The whole of the ground today was a complete swamp . . . . The whole surroundings are, in my opinion, in their present condition not only a nuisance and injurious to the health of those living on the land, but also to the people, and especially the children visiting the show.'

KING STREET, APPROACHING CROSS DEEP 1897 ZZZ05226 (Courtesy of LB Richmond-upon-Thames Local Studies Collection)

ORDNANCE SURVEY MAP SHOWING TWICKENHAM AND SURROUNDING AREAS 1912

CHAPTER FOUR

RIVERSIDE TOWN TO LONDON BOROUGH - TWICKENHAM IN THE 20TH CENTURY

A VIEW OF THE RIVER THAMES 1955 T91006

BY THE START of the 20th century, Twickenham had developed into a very different settlement from the picturesque riverside village beloved of artists two centuries earlier. The break-up of the old local estates and their redevelopment as mass-market housing had changed its pastoral character irretrievably. New technology was also making a dramatic impact on the appearance of the town. Trams and motorcars replaced horse-drawn transport, electricity arrived in 1902 to replace gas lighting, and tarmacadam came to the roads.

The town grew rapidly at the start of the 20th century. Between 1881 and 1911 the population increased from 12,500 to over 29,000 residents. Around 17,000 houses were built in the first ten years of the century. Trams arrived in the town in 1903. Cole's brewery in London Road was acquired by Brandon's of Putney in 1900 and closed down in 1927. Over the centuries the view of the River Thames from Richmond Hill was regarded as one of the most sublime views in England, and had inspired writers like Pope and painters like Kent. Garden historian Mavis Batey described it as 'the cradle of the English landscape movement'.

The break-up of the large Twickenham riverside estates at the turn of the 20th century, and the possibility of encroaching

TRAMS ON THE GREEN 1904 ZZZ05227 (Hazelle Jackson Collection)

urban development spoiling the celebrated view for ever, led to vociferous public concern and an 'indignation' campaign: 'The matchless Vale of the Thames with its goodly prospect spread around may soon be secured for the enjoyment and delight of the present and future generations for all time'. This turned out to be one of the earliest and most successful environmental campaigns of the 20th century. In 1902 the landscape on and below Richmond Hill became the first view to be protected in perpetuity by an Act of Parliament.

The council purchased Radnor House on Cross Deep for municipal offices in 1902. The Twickenham Park estate had already been redeveloped in the 19th century, and developers turned their sights on to Marble Hill on the banks of the Thames at East Twickenham.

A POSTCARD VIEW FROM RICHMOND HILL 1910
ZZZ05228 (Hazelle Jackson Collection)

Looking across the Thames Valley to Twickenham

RADNOR HOUSE FROM THE ROAD IN THE EARLY 20TH CENTURY ZZZ05229
(LB Richmond-upon-Thames Local Studies Collection)

Marble Hill House and grounds was purchased by William Cunard and his sons in 1888; they planned to demolish the house and put up a housing estate on the park. Even while the view from Richmond Hill was being saved in 1901, roads and sewers were being laid across Marble Hill preparatory to house-building. The access roads had already been laid for the development by the time London County Council, after strenuous local protest, purchased the estate in 1902 with the aid of public contributions at a cost of £72,000. It was formally opened to the public as a park on 30 May 1903.

A notable historic house was lost when Mount Lebanon, that stood in large grounds between Orleans House and York House, and was vacant in 1907, burnt down in 1909. The pilasters, balconies, staircase, stair rails, and marble mantlepieces were sold to Mr Paul Schweder, who installed them in his own residence - Courtlands House in Worthing. (Courtlands House is now owned by Bond International Software Corporation, who have restored it with the support of Worthing Council.) In 1906 William (Billy) Williams bought ten acres of market garden in Twickenham on behalf of the Rugby Football Union; this led to the ground's affectionate nickname 'Billy Williams's Cabbage Patch'.

MARBLE HILL HOUSE 2005 T91705k (Hazelle Jackson)

THE RUGBY GROUND

The original cost of the ten acres of market garden which Billy Williams purchased for the RFU in 1906 was £5,572 12s 6d. Two covered stands for 3,000 spectators each were built on the East and West sides of the pitch as well as a terrace on the South side for 7,000 spectators, and an open mound on the North side. A vehicle park for 200 cars and carriages was located behind the South stand. The total cost of these was £8,812 15s 0d, raised by debentures.

The pitch was raised above ground level to avoid flooding by the River Crane; drainage and fencing cost another £1,606 9s 4d. But on 2 October 1909 fewer than 2,000 people watched Harlequins beat Richmond 14-10. During the First World War the pitch was used as grazing for horses, cattle and sheep. In the Second World War the stadium was used as a civil defence depot, the East car park was dug up for allotments, and the West car park was a coal dump.

THE RUGBY GROUND c1960 T91046

The rugby stadium continued to develop throughout the 20th century, and by the end of the century had capacity for 75,000 spectators with plans for further expansion.

Not far from the new rugby ground, Dr Ralph Jupp set up his London Film Company in 1912 at St Margaret's in a former skating rink. In 1927 the studios were acquired by the Hamburg-born film producer Julius Hagen, and renamed Twickenham Film

Studios. Apart from interruptions during wartime, the studios are still in business today. One of the best-known films to be made there was the Beatles' first film 'A Hard Day's Night' (1964), directed by Richard Lester. Several outdoor scenes were shot locally, including Ringo Starr drinking in the Turk's Head pub, and all of the Beatles entering houses in Ailsa Road.

In 1908 Walter Hammerton (1881-1956), a local waterman, set up a small business hiring out boats from a boathouse on a pontoon opposite Marble Hill House. He also set up a ferry charging 1d a trip across the river to the Surrey bank. This initiative alarmed Lord Dysart who owned Twickenham Ferry, and William Champion the licensee, and in 1913 Lord Dysart took legal action to stop Hammerton's ferry. He lost his case in July 1915, and Hammerton's ferry still runs from the riverbank at Marble Hill park, only these days it uses an electric motor.

The original Twickenham Ferry continued to operate, with some breaks, until the 1970s. Patrick Doyle, of the York House Society, recalls that as a lad in the 1950s he used to go fishing with school friends in the early morning across the river in the gravel pits at Ham: 'We were

HAMMERTON'S FERRY 2004 T91709k (Hazelle Jackson)

TWICKENHAM FERRY 1910 ZZZ05230 (Hazelle Jackson Collection)

junior members of the Twickenham Piscatorial Society at the time. We would get up early and go down to the riverside at around 7 o'clock in the morning, and ring the bell to knock up the ferryman. He would get up, put on his great coat, and row the four of us and our bicycles over the river for around 1s 3d. Then we would cycle round to the flooded gravel pit and set up our rods.'

A complicated legal wrangle over access to the river from its traditional mooring caused the ferry to close for good in the early 1980s. The last ferryman was Dave Hastings, a former Royal Navy diver and an amiable, burly, red-headed man who was often accompanied by his son and dog. For years afterwards his wooden wherry, built to the original Tudor design, slowly rotted away on the slipway.

THE RUINED TWICKENHAM FERRY 2001
T91710k (Hazelle Jackson)

Fact File

The first Twickenham railway bridge over the Thames lasted less than 60 years. In 1891 a cast-iron railway bridge near Norbury Junction collapsed, causing considerable concern over the bridge across the Thames at Richmond, which had a similar design. A new bridge was completed in 1908 that used part of the old piers and abutments but had new decking and superstructure.

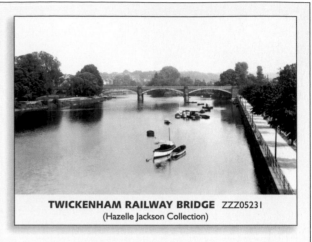

TWICKENHAM RAILWAY BRIDGE ZZZ05231
(Hazelle Jackson Collection)

In 1911 local residents celebrated the coronation of George V in great style with processions and parties on the green, but the shadow of war was lengthening and, like everywhere else in the Britain, the growth and prosperity of the town was brought to an abrupt halt by the outbreak of the First World War. Life was never to be the same again.

SHOPS ON HEATH ROAD DECORATED FOR THE CORONATION OF GEORGE V IN 1911
ZZZ05232 (Courtesy of LB Richmond-upon-Thames Local Studies Collection)

THE CORONATION PROCESSION UNDER THE DIP 1911 ZZZ05233
(Courtesy of LB Richmond-upon-Thames Local Studies Collection)

The impact on Twickenham of the carnage of the First World War can be seen by the many local names on the war memorials around the town and neighbouring districts. The statue in Radnor Gardens commemorates the soldiers who died for the cause of freedom.

After the war, small-scale industrial development took the place of the old market gardens, and housing continued to spread over the old estates as the population expanded.

In 1906, York House was sold to Sir Ratan Tata, a wealthy Indian merchant. His widow continued to live there for some years but eventually decided to return to India, and the house was put up for sale in 1924. The York House Society was formed to campaign for its preservation for the community, and Lady Tata sold it to the council for £20,580.

A further £39,000 was spent on fixtures, fittings and refurbishment.

THE WAR MEMORIAL IN RADNOR GARDENS 2005
T91711k (Hazelle Jackson)

YORK HOUSE STATUES

STATUARY AT YORK HOUSE c1955 T91019

The white marble statues of water nymphs, which form such a striking feature in the grounds of York House, were purchased in Rome in the late 19th century by the city financier Whitaker Wright - intended for the grotto room under the lake at his Witley Park estate in Surrey. They had not been unpacked when he committed suicide in 1904 after a financial scandal. The statues were then acquired by Sir Ratan Tata, the last private owner of York House, at a reported cost of £600 and installed in the gardens. The statues were restored in 1988 but need constant attention and protection from vandals to remain in good condition.

york house statuary appeal twickenham

AN APPEAL

To raise money for the restoration of the York House garden statues.

THE RESTORATION APPEAL LEAFLET 1987
ZZZ05234 (York House Society)

**THE OLD TOWN HALL, KING STREET,
BEING DEMOLISHED IN 1929** ZZZ05220
(Courtesy of LB Richmond-upon-Thames Local Studies Collection)

The old Town Hall in King Street was demolished
when the street was widened in 1929. York House
was then used as the new Town Hall.

Fact File

*Shapurji Saklatvala (1874-1936) who was the third Indian
person and the second member of the Communist Party to
become a British MP, lived in Twickenham in the early 20th
century. Shapurji Saklatvala was born in Bombay in 1874,
a member of the wealthy Tata clan (Sir Ratan Tata of York
House was his cousin). In 1905 he was sent to England from
India for medical treatment; by 1907 he was involved in left
wing politics in the UK.*

*Saklatvala worked as Sir Ratan Tata's personal assistant,
and the Saklatvala family lived nearby at 51, Lebanon Park.
His daughter, Sehri, has recalled how Ratan Tata, who had
no children of his own, 'made a big fuss of Shapur's increasing
brood … they enjoyed playing in the spacious gardens of York
House; especially the Japanese garden with its miniature trees
and slender bridge over a little stream.'*

*Saklatvala supported a number of left wing causes in Britain,
including conscientious objectors, who used to meet in each
other's houses. In 1921, he joined the Communist Party and
became the party's candidate the next year in North Battersea.
With the support of the Battersea Trades Council, Saklatvala
won the seat in the 1922 general election, losing it by 186 votes
in the 1923 election and regaining it by 540 votes in the 1924
election. During the general strike in 1926 he was a strong
supporter of the Miners' Federation. In the 1929 elections the
Labour Party withdrew its support for communist candidates
and he lost the seat and did not regain it.*

SHAPURJI SAKLATVALA
ZZZ05235 (Courtesy of Sehri Saklatvala)

Quotations from 'The Fifth
Commandment' - the biography
of Shapurji Saklatvala by his
daughter Sehri Saklatvala.
Reproduced with permission.

In 1924, Richmond House, a large house with extensive grounds on the river-front by the Embankment, came into council ownership, following an unsuccessful bid at auction, a fumbled attempt at compulsory purchase, and a public inquiry.

There was opposition to the purchase; local people feared that demolition would follow, and the land be developed for public buildings. This was true, the council wanted the land for '... road improvements, public offices, a fire station, baths and washhouses and sanitary conveniences.' It was demolished in the late 1920s, and the municipal swimming baths were built on the site in the 1930s. King Street was widened in 1928 when the old Town Hall was demolished.

In 1882 the Orleans estate had been purchased by William Cunard, the shipping magnate, who later purchased Marble Hill House for development. After his death, his widow continued to live there but the house had been empty for several years after the First World War when it was sold to the Crane River Sand and Ballast Company. The new owners sold off the remaining furniture and fittings at auction on 3 March 1926, rapidly demolished the house, and started gravel extraction on the site - eventually removing over 200,000 tons of sand and gravel.

Local resident the Hon Mrs Nelly Levy (later Ionides), the daughter of Shell Oil magnate Lord Bearsted, set out to save the rest of the estate. She purchased the Octagon and adjacent wings, the extensive stable block, and Riverside House (next door to Orleans House). After buying Orleans House, she contributed £2,500 towards the total of £10,000 needed by the corporation to acquire Orleans Gardens.

A VIEW OF KING STREET, SHOWING TROLLEYBUSES AND THE ODEON 1955 T91021

THE OCTAGON

In the early 1960s Mrs Ionides bequeathed the Octagon, Riverside House and her collection of paintings to the local authority. In 1972 the Orleans House Gallery opened, and is now the venue for varied exhibitions, including displays of paintings from the Ionides collection. There are a number of paintings in the permanent collection at Orleans House Gallery inspired by the view from and towards Richmond Hill.

THE OCTAGON AT ORLEANS HOUSE 2005
T91712k (Hazelle Jackson)

The gardens were used as the site for Orleans Park Secondary School in the 1970s, and all that now remains of the once celebrated landscape is a small garden next to the Octagon Gallery where the original house stood. A more unexpected fate awaited Riverside House, which had formed part of the original Ionides bequest to the corporation. Mrs Ionides's granddaughter, the photographer Camilla Jessel, married the distinguished Polish composer Andrzej Panufnik in 1963. As a wedding present, her parents bought a long lease on Riverside House for the couple. In the 1980s and 1990s successive governments enacted a number of changes to property law, entitling council tenants and leaseholders to buy their own homes. Lady Panufnik applied to exercise her right to purchase Riverside House and, after taking legal advice, the council reluctantly granted her the right to buy. The sale was completed in 2004 for £1.38m. The council announced that the proceeds were to be invested in the Octagon Trust to benefit the local community in accordance with the bequest of Mrs Ionides.

Twickenham obtained its charter as a borough in 1926, and York House was officially opened as the Town Hall for Twickenham Borough Council by the Duke of York (later George VI) on 16 November 1926.

CHARTER DAY IN KING STREET 1926 ZZZ05236 (Courtesy of LB Richmond-upon-Thames Local Studies Collection)

Twickenham Park House, a substantial early Victorian house built near the earlier house in 1829, also fell prey to gravel extraction in the 1920s. Contemporary photographs show it standing isolated in the middle of flooded gravel pits in the late 1920s. It was demolished in 1929, and the site was filled in and used for semi-detached houses in the 1930s. Today it the site of Park House Gardens. More building in the late 1920s also took place in the Whitton area. Developers bought up the old estates, and laid them out in a more modern development to accommodate the new middle and working class population of the town. Between 1920 and 1937, 975 council houses were built.

The first trolleybuses are fondly recalled by resident Cliff Hall: 'As someone who grew up in Twickenham in the 1940s-50s, I used trollybuses often to go to school. I really do miss this splendid form of transport. Pollution-free and silent-running, something that our transport system is very short of these days. My stepfather, who spent all of his working life at Fulwell depot, drove the first Diddler into service in May 1931.'

By 1931 there were nearly 40,000 people in the area of the old parish. In 1937 the urban district councils of Teddington, Hampton, and Hampton Wick merged with Twickenham, and in 1951 there were over 61,000 residents.

The town's original swimming pool was built in Mereway in 1896, and used for many years before closing due to pollution of the water. As part of providing civic local facilities, the council erected a large open-air swimming pool in the town centre in the 1930s on the site of Richmond House, between King Street and the river. The site was purchased with a loan from the Ministry of Health, for the express purpose of providing public walks and pleasure grounds. A splendid art-deco lido with fountains and a cafe area was opened in the late 1935, the year of King George VI's Silver Jubilee.

Building continued in and around the town in the 1930s. London Road was altered in the 1930s when Fortescue House, where Regal House stands today, was pulled down. Poulett Lodge, formerly the home of Earl Poulett at the top of Cross Deep, was demolished in 1933 and replaced with a block of flats, called Thames Eyot.

Another flurry of house-building took place out towards Whitton after local Councillor Wills lost his battle to save the Duke of Argyll's estate. Fulwell Park, home to the exiled King Manoel II of Portugal in the early 20th century, was developed by the firm Wates, and roads in the Fulwell Park estate area reflect the Portuguese connections of the area.

LONDON ROAD c1955 T91022

'L' TYPE HOUSE

The house illustrated contains: Entrance Hall, large Dining-room - Kitchenette with French windows looking on to Garden, Drawing-room, Tiled Bathroom with chromiumplated fittings, Three Bedrooms. Also available with two Bedrooms.

From : £425 FREEHOLD

£12:10 TOTAL DEPOSIT
FROM 9/9 WEEKLY

Now is your opportunity to buy a really up-to-date labour-saving home with a total deposit of only **£12.10.0.** Only a few houses at Twickenham, Sidcup and Barnehurst are available on these exceptional terms, so do not delay. If you cannot call at an estate during the next day or so send coupon for full details.

TWICKENHAM

GROSVENOR PARK ESTATE is only a few minutes from shops, schools, churches, cinemas, etc. and is most easily reached from Feltham or Twickenham Stations which are connected by a frequent service of Southern Electric trains with Waterloo. Our saloon cars are always waiting at both Stations to convey you round the estate free of charge and without obligation. Phone: Feltham 2403.

SIDCUP (ALBANY PARK)

ALBANY PARK ESTATE is actually built adjacent to the new Southern Railway Station which is opening later this year. The Station is to be named after the estate. In the meantime come to Sidcup Southern Electric Station, 10 miles from London. Cars always await you. Albany Park is only a few minutes' walk from Bus Routes 132, 21, 51, 228 and 407. Phone: Sidcup 1471.

BARNEHURST

HILLCREST ESTATE is built amid the orchards on healthy high land overlooking the famous Golf Course. To visit this pleasant estate take the Southern Electric train from Charing Cross, Cannon St., or London Bridge to Barnehurst Station, 29 minutes. Cars always waiting. Phone: Erith 609.

NEW IDEAL HOMESTEADS
BRITAIN'S BEST & BIGGEST BUILDERS

'NEW IDEAL' SERVICES TO PURCHASERS

* Insurance covering the repayments.
* No road or legal charges.
* Insurance against Fatal Accident.
* All roads and pavements made.
* Every Home Fully Guaranteed.
* Mortgage Interest reduced to 4½%.

Show Houses on estates open daily until 9 p.m. Sundays included. Models at 62 Strand, W.C.2 (near Tivoli), and 26 Royal Exchange, E.C. 3 (opp. Bank), and at office adjoining Platform 16, Waterloo Station where free Rail Vouchers are obtainable.

COUPON FOR PARTICULARS

To New Ideal Homesteads, Ltd., 62, Strand, W.C.2. Phone: Temple Bar 6968. Send me details of buying a house with £12.10 deposit.

Name ....
Address ....
....
.............................D.H.7.5.35
I am interested in .... Estate

HOUSE ADVERTISEMENT 1934
ZZZ05237 (From a contemporary newspaper)

was constructed in the early 1930s and smashed across the end of the St Margaret's Trust Grounds, dividing them from the rest of the old Twickenham Park estate. The construction of the road was part of the major arterial road-building programme, which accompanied the rapid urban growth of London between the First and Second World Wars.

Twickenham Bridge was built by Maxwell Ayrton, and was one of three bridges opened on the same day in 1933 by the Prince of Wales (later Edward VIII). The arches in the bridge, constructed in 1932, have permanent hinges that allow them to adjust to changes of temperature. This was the first reinforced-concrete bridge in Britain constructed to this design.

Development in the town was halted by the Second World War in 1939. The first bomb fell on Hampton on 24 August 1940, destroying a house; from then on the town was bombed continuously until May 1941, with the National Physical Research Laboratory in Teddington a key target.

By now there was an urgent need to get traffic over the Thames on a modern road raid. The Great Chertsey Road (A316)

CHERTSEY ROAD IN THE 1930s ZZZ05238 (Author's Collection)

BOMB DAMAGE AT CROSS DEEP 1940 ZZZ05239 (Courtesy of LB Richmond-upon-Thames Local Studies Collection)

On 16 September 1940 a bomb scored a direct hit on Radnor House. The bomb fell straight through the empty house into the cellars, and witnesses reported that the house imploded. Today the grounds are used as a public park. This area of Cross Deep was particularly affected by bomb damage, leading to the demolition of houses between Radnor House and Ryan House including Cross Deep Hall and River Deep. The property known as Pope's garden had to be demolished after it suffered severe bomb damage.

By the end of July 1944 a total of 7,000 women and children had been evacuated. After the war ended in 1945, official

Fact File

Radnor House was destroyed by a direct hit from a German bomb in 1940. Several other houses nearby in Cross Deep were also destroyed by bombs. The bombardment of the town continued into the winter of November 1940, destroying 150 houses, damaging another 350 badly, and causing damage to a further 6,000 homes. Nine 500kg high explosive bombs were also dropped on the National Physical Laboratory. In 1944–45 the V-1s (doodlebugs) arrived followed by V-2 rockets.

statistics showed that 654 properties had to be pulled down, with 42 historic buildings and 29,000 other properties damaged. Downstream on the western side of the Chertsey Road, St Margaret's House, by then home to the Royal Naval College for Girls, was also destroyed by a bomb in 1940.

After the war Gordon House and the site of St Margaret's House were taken over by the Maria Grey Training College; this merged with the Borough Road Training College and Chiswick Polytechnic in 1975 to become the West London Institute of Higher Education. In 1995, the West London Institute was absorbed into Brunel University whose main campus is in Uxbridge.

In 1954 the old railway station buildings (where the car park is today outside the Albany) were replaced by the present booking office on London Road, and the platforms moved up to the other side of the road. Also scheduled for redevelopment was the remaining old part of the town between Church Street and the river, which had suffered bomb damage in the war.

In the 1950s, Middlesex County Council planners were asked to draw up a plan for renovation of the embankment and Church Street area by the Ministry of Town and Country Planning. Predictably, the planners came up with a scheme for knocking down most of Church Street and replacing it with flats (the proposed scheme would also have included demolishing the Queen's Head and the Fox Inn, and straightening the street). This scheme caused dismay beyond the confines of the town, in a row reminiscent of the one in 2005 over plans to knock down Victorian housing in Liverpool and replace it with modern housing stock.

KING STREET c1960 T91038

THE BARMY ARMS (FORMERLY THE QUEEN'S HEAD) 2004 T91713k (Hazelle Jackson)

Objections were raised by well-known figures like Sir John Betjeman and architectural historian Marc Girouard, who wrote that the proposed scheme was 'a classic example of how not to plan, for with steamroller simplicity planners would have knocked down virtually every house in the area to be replaced by blocks of flats ... not unnaturally local opinion reacted violently to this unfortunate plan ...' The (unnamed) planners, as might have been anticipated, responded 'we think our plan is sound. The old houses are boarded up and have been condemned anyway'.

As a result of the outcry a revised scheme was adopted, and The Richmond and Twickenham Times was able to report in June 1955: 'It was obvious, from a conference at York House on Tuesday, that organisations which have fought Middlesex County Council's plan for rebuilding the Church Street area of Twickenham have won an almost complete victory, as it is generally agreed that the new plans meet practically all the objections to the original plan.'

A further planning battle took place in the 1960s when the council wanted to knock down the end of Church Street in order to expand its offices on to the site. Some destruction took place in 1963 when the end of the street was cleared, including the demolition of the former Sawyers public house at the junction of Church Street and Church Lane, later known as Russell's Corner after the Russell cycle and motor engineering works established there in the 1920s.

CHURCH STREET 1974 ZZZ05250
(Courtesy of LB Richmond-upon-Thames Local Studies Collection)

In 1965, the municipal borough of Twickenham was merged with those of Barnes and Richmond (against the wishes of many residents) to become the London Borough of Richmond-upon-Thames under the umbrella of the Greater London Council. The town's maturity into suburbia was complete. The population, after a brief dip in the middle of the 20th century, started to grow yet again as developers and planners found ways to squeeze even more housing into the borough to meet the demand.

The new commuting population put increasing pressure on the roads. The M3 motorway was constructed in stages during 1970-90 in order to alleviate the severe congestion that had developed in the area. The Surrey section joining the A316 was opened in 1974; that year Clifden House, on the junction of Heath Road and Clifden Road, was the last old house in the town centre to be demolished.

There were several cinemas at the start of the 20th century, including the Lyric Palace cinema which opened in 1911 opposite York House on Richmond Road, and later became a Gaumont. In 1929, the Luxor cinema opened at the junction of Heath Road and Cross Deep where the houses called The Grove had stood in the 18th century; seating 1,700, it could accommodate a symphony orchestra, and had a John Compton theatre organ, and a well-equipped stage with a 40-foot proscenium. In the 1950s, the organ was wheeled onto the stage for the Saturday morning children's matinee, when Ena Baga would play her signature tune - 'Smoke Gets in Your Eyes'. One morning as she was playing this tune at the matinee, the stage tabs caught fire and started to smoke!

RICHMOND ROAD, THE GAUMONT CINEMA c1955 T91013

Fact File

When it opened in 1929, the usherettes at the Luxor Cinema were dressed in costumes inspired by Queen Cleopatra. The Luxor was eventually sold to the Odeon chain in 1944. By the time it closed in 1981, it was the only surviving cinema in the town; and when it was demolished to make way for redevelopment five years later, the town lost its last cinema. After a hotly contested planning application, the site was developed for its current use as a billiards hall, flats and shops. By the end of the 20th century all the local cinemas had been replaced by later developments, and residents had to cross the bridge to Richmond to visit the cinema.

Eel Pie Island is now a sleepy residential backwater for boat builders and residents, accessible via a footbridge from the embankment but, until the 1970s, the hotel on the island played host to a variety of activities. From jazz to R n' B, some of the rock greats who played in the Island Hotel at the start of their careers in the 1960s included the Rolling Stones, Rod Stewart, Pink Floyd, The Who, and Genesis.

One of the most memorable aspects of getting on to the island in its early days was the lack of a footbridge from the mainland until the mid 1950s. Before then, access was via an old chain ferry; if the ferry was not available, drunken revellers were sometimes known to swim back. Once the bridge was installed, it was a regular occurrence to see a band's transit lorry stuck on the bridge.

The original Island club closed down in 1967, but was reopened in 1969 as Colonel Barefoot's Rock Garden. A suspicious fire demolished the empty hotel in 1972, and a block of flats went up in its place. Today the island is home to inventor Trevor Bayliss, the rowing club, a variety of quaint houses, several boatyards, and a nature reserve.

A POSTCARD OF THE ISLAND HOTEL 1911 ZZZ05241 (Hazelle Jackson Collection)

EEL PIE ISLAND FOOTBRIDGE

An early view of the bridge to Eel Pie Island

THE RIVERSIDE c1955 T91055

In 1988, the old concrete footbridge to Eel Pie Island was replaced by a new one designed by Stuart Holdsworth. Delivered in two sections, it was built on a barge, then floated round the island and positioned by the fall of the tide. Due to the light structure, compensating weights suspended on rods under the centre section remove unwanted bounce when crossing. These were adjusted on site to obtain the correct frequency.

THE EEL PIE ISLAND BRIDGE, REBUILT IN 1988
ZZZ05262 (Hazelle Jackson)

Prince Charles visited Twickenham in 1981 as part of its 900-year-old celebrations. However, local feeling was that the town centre lost its way during the 1980s as developers and property speculators moved in to exploit the rising land values. They had little sympathy for the distinctive history and atmosphere of the town, or the wishes of the local community.

The loss of the local ice rink to development for luxury housing in the 1990s aroused very strong feelings. The rink originally opened in 1928 as the Sports Drome on the Twickenham side of the river, formerly Twickenham Meadows. In 1987, the owners sold it to property developers for housing. Assurances were made to anxious residents by the developers and members of the council that, if planning permission were granted, a replacement £22.5m sports centre with a new ice rink would be built elsewhere in the borough. The plans were greeted by widespread local scepticism, and aroused fierce local opposition including a petition of 48,000 signatures from local residents supported by the local MPs.

However, the scheme was approved by the council, and a vast luxury housing estate went up in the 1990s. It emerged that the council had reached an agreement with the developers in September 1989, not made public at the time. This agreement was that if a suitable new site for the new ice rink could not be found, the developers would pay the council compensation of £2.2 million - and that is what happened. The town was left without an ice rink, and the money was absorbed into the council's budget. Many local residents felt the Liberal-Democrat controlled council had been less than frank about negotiations, failed to negotiate effectively, and lost them their ice rink. Local Richmond campaigner Richard Meacock continues to press for a new ice rink in the borough.

In 1986, another controversy erupted over the sale by the council of 212 acres of public

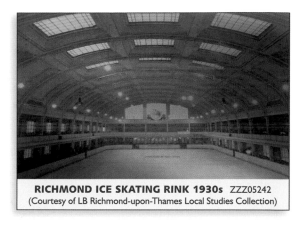

RICHMOND ICE SKATING RINK 1930s ZZZ05242
(Courtesy of LB Richmond-upon-Thames Local Studies Collection)

land on a 999-year lease that was occupied by Fulwell Golf Course and Squires Garden Centre. Subsequently it was found that between 1982 and 1983 the four acres occupied by the Garden Centre had had their Metropolitan Open Land status removed, for reasons that were never uncovered. This change in status, which would have significantly increased the value of the land, was not made known at the time of the sale to council members, or to the surveyor retained by the council to value the land. The sale went through in 1986 at the original valuation price as though it were still MOL status land. When the change in status emerged, this caused a big row locally that has rumbled on ever since.

In 2005, a Scrutiny Task Force set up by the Council to investigate the circumstances of the sale, uncovered a trail of missing, non-existent and misfiled documents, and concluded: 'The Task Group's finding do give them cause for concern and an understanding of why some members of the public believe the council was at the very least unprofessional/incompetent.'

Residents continued to take an active interest in the arts and music. In 1981, the

Richmond Shakespeare Society opened in the Mary Wallace Theatre in the converted 1870 Mission Hall on the embankment. It now presents eight productions of traditional and modern plays each year. St Mary's new church hall is also in regular demand for talks and lectures by local arts and study groups.

In 1987, the south-east of England experienced its worst storm since 1703. Earlier in the evening in response to a viewer's phone call, TV meteorologist, and East Twickenham resident, Michael Fish had announced on national television: 'A lady has rung in to ask if there is going to be a hurricane tonight - there is not!' Later that night the storm arrived with winds gusting at over 100 miles per hour in some places. A Sealink cross-channel ferry was blown ashore at Folkestone, and over 15 million trees were felled. The storm hit the town hard with trees uprooted and falling on houses, cars and roads. Nearby Kew Gardens lost about one-third of its trees.

One local resident recalled afterwards: 'We were woken in the night by howling winds and so much noise. There was a great roaring noise outside in the blackness and all the lights went out. The window frames shook so violently I thought the windows would cave in and my brother in Surrey phoned later to say the wind had ripped all the tiles off his roof. The next morning the street outside our house resembled a war zone.'

A FLIER FOR THE RICHMOND SHAKESPEARE SOCIETY 2005 ZZZ05243

THE GREAT STORM, RIVERSIDE 1987 ZZZ05244 (Hazelle Jackson)

THE GREAT STORM, RIVERSIDE 1987 ZZZ05245 (Hazelle Jackson)

In the 1980s Richmond-upon-Thames, on the south bank of the river, was given a new lease of life with a sympathetic mixed-use development on the waterfront, designed by the neo-classical architect Quinlan Terry. Visitors flooded into the town to enjoy the theatre, a fashionable mix of smart boutiques, restaurants, and multi-screen cinema complexes.

Local property companies set rents for retail premises in Twickenham town centre at levels derived from the high rents achieved in neighbouring Richmond, and by reference to the high cost of housing locally. In practice, the anticipated demand from the big national chains of shops or luxury stores was just not there, and smaller specialist shops could not afford the rents being asked. With the notable exception of Church Street, where some small specialist shops did survive, parts of the town centre took on a rather melancholy appearance with a surfeit of boarded-up shops, building societies and charity shops.

During this period Twickenham had lost several of its leisure facilities - cinema, swimming baths, and ice rink - after hotly contested planning decisions, which pitched councillors and senior town hall staff against local residents. The Odeon cinema was pulled down in the 1980s and replaced by a billiard hall and 'mixed-use' development; the swimming baths on Twickenham Embankment were closed in 1981 and never re-opened, and the ice rink in East Twickenham was demolished and replaced by luxury housing in the 1990s.

YORK HOUSE GARDENS c1955 T91014

THE THAMES c1955 T91003

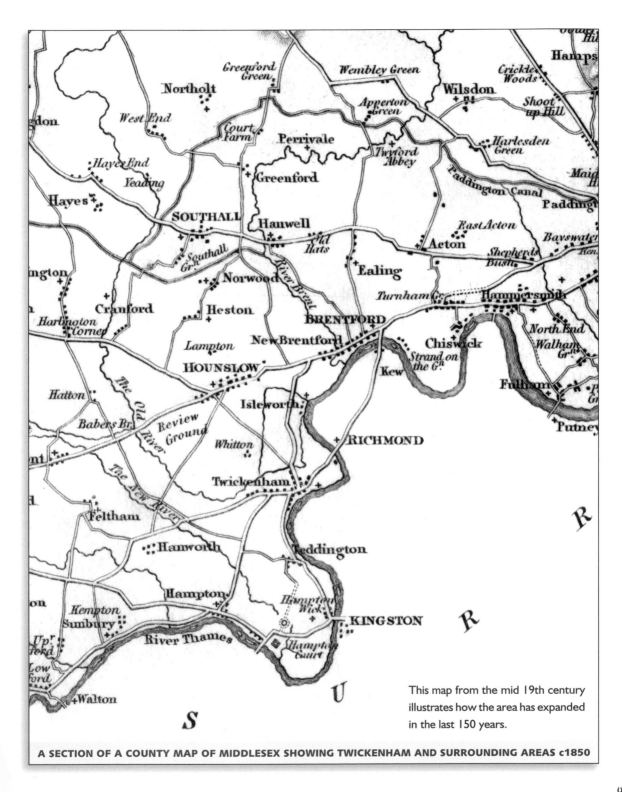

This map from the mid 19th century illustrates how the area has expanded in the last 150 years.

A SECTION OF A COUNTY MAP OF MIDDLESEX SHOWING TWICKENHAM AND SURROUNDING AREAS c1850

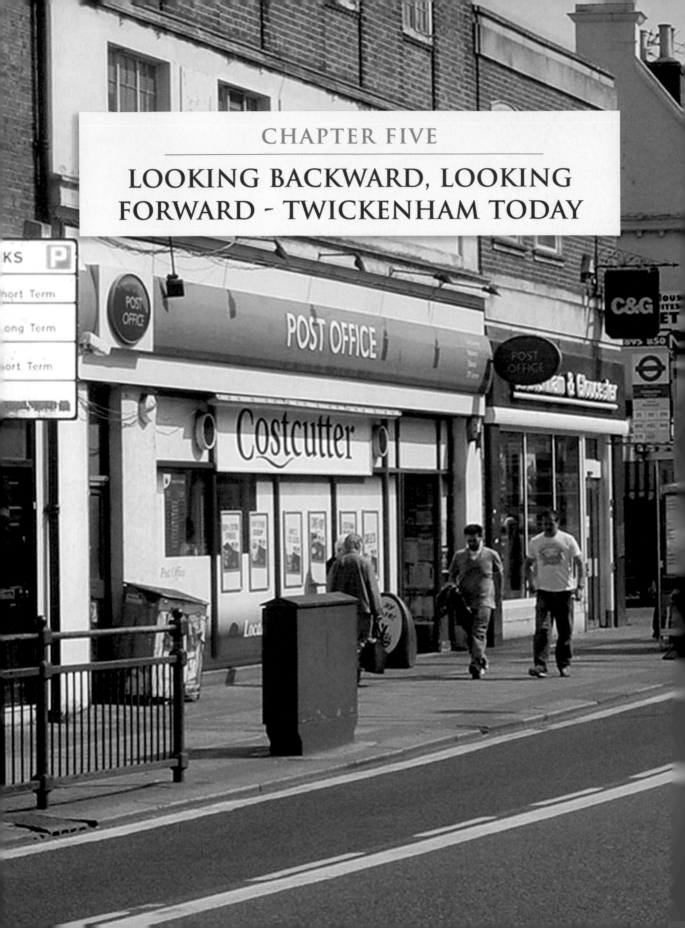

CHAPTER FIVE

LOOKING BACKWARD, LOOKING FORWARD - TWICKENHAM TODAY

THE CENTRE c1960 T91039

BY THE START OF the new millennium, Twickenham had evolved a long way from the idyllic Arcadian village of the 18th century with its elegant riverside mansions and villas set in sylvan grounds. Today it is a mix of predominantly Victorian and 1930s housing interspersed with post-modern infill development, and in 1965 it was subsumed by the post-war growth of London into the London Borough of Richmond-upon-Thames. Overhead the planes roar ceaselessly into Heathrow airport. The traffic below queues to navigate the town centre, where the River Thames glides almost unseen behind the 1930s shops of King Street and the suburban villas along Cross Deep. The town centre's shops and restaurants sprawl along Heath Road to the Green.

Yet modern Twickenham has many attractions: good transport links; parks and leafy green spaces; good schools; proximity to the river Thames; and a large stock of spacious 19th- and early 20th-century housing. All these factors make it a popular choice with middle-class commuters, and have brought a new and lively population to the town. Residents celebrated the new millennium

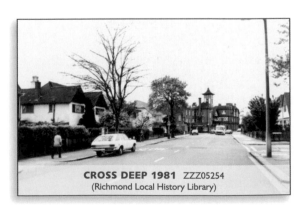

CROSS DEEP 1981 ZZZ05254
(Richmond Local History Library)

with a series of street parties. Thirteen of these around the rugby stadium were sponsored by the Rugby Football Union as part of its good-neighbour policy. Generally though, the celebrations were low-key compared to earlier centuries with their street processions, marching bands and bunting.

During the late 20th century and up to the present day, central government has increased its control over local government finance nationally, so cash-strapped local authorities have found it increasingly difficult to balance the books. The London Borough of Richmond-upon-Thames found itself disadvantaged under local government financial policies adopted by successive Conservative and New-Labour governments, and needing to maximise its assets. Over the years the borough, in common with many others, had acquired a number of attractive sites, which, as the housing market heated up, attracted the attentions of developers and house builders, notably the old swimming baths on Twickenham Riverside.

The stage was thus set for the biggest and most controversial planning battle in Twickenham in the last 30 years: the development of the former municipal swimming baths site, on the embankment overlooking the Thames in central Twickenham.

THE TERRACE, YORK HOUSE c1955 T91018

THE RIVERSIDE c1965 T91054

After the baths closed in 1981, officially for refurbishment, the council decided that the demand for a new pool could not justify the cost of extensive repair or replacement, and a search began for a new use for the site. During the 1980s and 1990s a succession of proposals, rejections, counter-proposals, appeals, inquiries and discussions took place with various developers and the local population, but no agreement could be reached. The council favoured controlled development by the private sector, but local amenity groups were adamant that the area should be preserved for public access and enjoyment. Meanwhile the baths were left to decay into a derelict eyesore.

By early 2002 the Liberal Democrat-controlled council, frustrated by years of failed development plans, were very keen to see the site developed by the private sector in a scheme which, it argued, would deliver financial and leisure benefits to local residents. The Twickenham Riverside Terrace Group (a umbrella group of local amenity societies) strenuously opposed this proposal, and argued strongly that as all the land was originally purchased as public amenity land, it should remain in public hands to benefit the local community. They put forward proposals for an alternative scheme for the site to remain a community space.

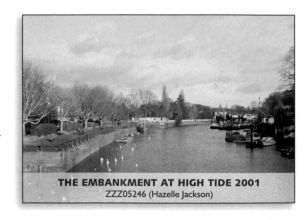

THE EMBANKMENT AT HIGH TIDE 2001
ZZZ05246 (Hazelle Jackson)

Richmond Council, despite vociferous local opposition, struck a deal to sell the site to their preferred developers, the property group Dawnay Day, who own most of the shops and flats on the south side of King Street, adjoining the old baths site. The deal involved the council selling their land to Dawnay Day on a 125-year lease, in exchange for a peppercorn rent and a substantial payment towards leisure in the borough and some access to the facilities on the site. Councillors and Council staff vigorously argued that this represented a good deal for residents and for the site.

Local residents remained resolutely unconvinced. There were objections that the terms of the deal were inequitable, that the development proposed was unattractive, too large and unsympathetic to the riverside site, that the proposed access to the new onsite leisure facilities offered was unsatisfactory

YORK HOUSE, NOW THE COUNCIL OFFICES c1965 T91056

and, in the case of the Twickenham Riverside Terrace Group, that the riverside site was a public open space. There were also concerns over whether in future the developers might exercise a right to buy the freehold of the site, which would then be lost to public ownership forever. Meanwhile the baths, once a splendid art deco lido, continued to be vandalised and deteriorate.

THE RIVER AND THE PARISH CHURCH c1955 T91002

In the local elections of 2002, the Liberal Democrats lost control of the council to the Conservatives after nineteen years in power. The incoming Tory council had campaigned on reviewing the latest plans for the baths site, which had been approved by the Liberal Democrats shortly before they lost office.

After this review, the Conservative-run council terminated negotiations with Dawnay Day in July 2002. Councillor Tony Arbour, leader of the council, stated: 'Having explored this matter in detail, I firmly believe that the cabinet's decision is in the best interests of the people of Richmond-upon-Thames. I look forward to receiving the September report, and to selecting an option for redevelopment which will bring the troubled history of this site to an end. My administration will work to ensure that this site will be something that future generations can be proud of.'

An interim scheme was developed in 2004. This involved demolition of the baths and landscaping an area of land at the western end of the site as a public open space. The bath site was finally cleared in late 2004, and the new park was formally opened on 1 June 2005 by the mayor Councillor Robin Jowit. Two weeks later the area was thronged with crowds enjoying the sunshine and its riverside location for the Twickenham Festival.

The long-term future of the entire site had still to be decided in the summer of 2005. The Jubilee Gardens are scheduled to last until 2009. In 2004 the government inspector's report on the local Unitary Development Plan, where it referred to the baths site, included a recommendation that the former swimming pool site should be predominately a public open space 'immutably'. In 2005 the council announced that work was to start on a

THE DEMOLITION OF THE OLD MUNICIPAL SWIMMING BATHS 2004 T91715k (Hazelle Jackson)

JUBILEE GARDENS

On 1 June 2005 the Jubilee Gardens was formally opened by the mayor, Councillor Robin Jowit, on the western side of the old swimming baths site. It has a small Japanese style garden with seating at river level, and a children's playground and cafe on the upper terrace.

THE OPENING OF THE JUBILEE GARDENS 2005 ZZZ05247 (Hazelle Jackson)

planning brief for the long-term future of the site: 'A planning application for the site will be made in 2007 with the aim of proceeding with further development of the site in 2009. It is intended that the development will include a commercial element: housing (including affordable housing), cafe and restaurants, and possibly some retail space.' In March 2005 the Twickenham Riverside Terrace Group posted a rallying cry on its web site: 'The Council's future plans are not known but ... we shall continue to fight to restore this open space to the local community in accordance with its purchase in 1924 for "public walks and pleasure purposes".'

The year 2002 marked the 50th anniversary of Queen Elizabeth II's accession to the throne, and a range of celebrations took place around the country to mark the occasion. On a fine sunny day on 25 June, the Queen and Prince Phillip met a large number of local school children and charity groups at a 'Picnic in the Park' in Bushy Park organised by Susannah Moore of the London Borough of Richmond-upon-Thames. More than 40,000 members of the public joined in the celebrations that included an events arena, displays, bands, and a variety of stalls and exhibitions.

Twickenham's town centre managers worked hard throughout this period to promote the town. In 1996 the Twickenham Festival was started with street music, street markets, tours of local historic houses, and dragon boat-racing on the Thames during a two-week-long celebration of the town and its history. In 2000 a regular farmers' market started on the Holly Road car park (the site of the Poppe rubber factory until the 1980s) on Saturday mornings. Regular French farmers' markets in Church Street have also proved a popular local attraction. The annual fair on Twickenham Green became a popular venue for residents and their children.

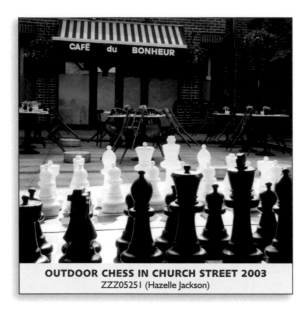

OUTDOOR CHESS IN CHURCH STREET 2003
ZZZ05251 (Hazelle Jackson)

Although the old Island Hotel on Eel Pie Island has long gone, the musical traditions of the town remain strong with many local pubs and wine bars offering live music. In 2000, the Eel Pie Club was founded in the Cabbage Patch pub in London Road to 'preserve and continue the heritage of Richmond Rhythm & Blues in the area where it all began in the 1960s - Eel Pie Island.' A museum for Richmond and Twickenham Rhythm 'n' Blues memorabilia was set up in the pub and a number of venerable old rock musicians have been spotted playing at local venues around the town.

THE TWICKENHAM FESTIVAL, CHURCH STREET 2005 T91716k (Hazelle Jackson)

KING STREET, THE GEORGE INN 2005
T91717k (Hazelle Jackson)

In 2003, a new planning row broke out over plans by Richmond College, the local tertiary college (which is actually in Twickenham) to fund expansion plans by selling off part of their site in Crane Valley for housing. The local MP, Vincent Cable, was drawn into the debate and spoke on behalf of residents, saying 'since the council appears to share residents' concerns, it must vote down aggressive development proposals which create large numbers of new houses encroaching on open land and generating substantial additional traffic on local roads'. In 2005 the council responded by publishing new planning guidelines for the Crane Valley, whose stated aims were to ensure all new development 'is compatible in scale and character with the local area, minimising any adverse impacts'.

Other targets for local amenity societies and residents' groups have included the expansion of Heathrow airport and its night flights, the erection of mobile phone masts, and the need to upgrade Mogden sewage works.

All these developments have welded the local communities into a formidable fighting force in many parts of the borough. IT-literate residents communicate via the internet to co-ordinate their protests, and residents' groups hire professionals to make their case at meetings where they fight to preserve the local heritage and environment.

Campaigns to clean up the riverside are enthusiastically supported and volunteer conservationists meet regularly intervals to clean up the riverbed at low tide and remove litter and unsightly vegetation from the tow paths and adjoining common land. Recycling is also well supported locally with the London Borough of Richmond-upon-Thames leading the way nationally.

THE SITE OF THE FORMER ODEON CINEMA ON THE CORNER OF CROSS DEEP AND HEATH ROAD 2005 T91714k (Hazelle Jackson)

THE RIVERBED CLEAN-UP 2004 ZZZ05249 (Hazelle Jackson)

As the UK population crept towards 60 million, property developers and house builders had to search for less likely sites. Large houses, even old coaching inns, were converted into flats, and new housing squeezed into ever-smaller gaps in residential areas. In 2002 Brunel University sold its 14-acre London campus (the old Twickenham Park estate) to upmarket housing developers Octagon in a multi-million pound deal. By 2005 the first luxury houses in a development, called Richmond Lock, were ready for occupation; its larger houses were snapped up eagerly at prices over £1m. The rising house prices led to a shortage of affordable homes locally for low-paid workers such as young school-teachers.

The Rugby Stadium's continued expansion has attracted greater numbers to its increasingly busy programme throughout the year, thus causing larger crowds in the town centre. Taking bottles or cans into the ground for matches is banned, and this has generated a significant increase in the number of bars and restaurants in the town. Many of the town's older premises have undergone a facelift recently while others, including the old post office in London Road, have been converted into wine bars. Match days are heavily policed, but the increased number of drinking establishments has increased the number of inebriated youths at weekends,

arousing local concern.

In 2004 the local police started to make greater use of antisocial-behaviour orders (ASBOs) to tackle offenders. Chief Superintendent Edwards told the local press: 'We will not tolerate antisocial behaviour and will make good use of fixed penalty notices too. We will not tolerate persistent trouble makers who blight our towns.' The council announced a crackdown on graffiti, with rewards offered to those reporting the miscreants and leading to a conviction.

OCTAGON'S RICHMOND LOCK DEVELOPMENT 2005 T91718k (Hazelle Jackson)

THE OLD POST OFFICE, LONDON ROAD 2005 T91719k (Hazelle Jackson)

LOOKING UP KING STREET 2005 T91720k (Hazelle Jackson)

KING STREET c1965 T91037

In 2002, a century after the passing of the landmark 1902 Act of Parliament that protected the view from Richmond Hill, the focus was firmly back on restoring and conserving the historic Thames landscape in south-west London. Originally inspired by architect and Richmond resident, Kim Wilkie, the 'Thames Landscape Strategy: Hampton to Kew' is an ambitious multi-million-pound project to restore the vistas and avenues linking the landscapes in the twelve-mile stretch of river.

As part of the Arcadia-in-the-City project, views across the Thames in Marble Hill Park and Radnor Gardens have been restored by the removal of self-sown trees and scrub to reveal the original 18th-century vistas.

In December 2004 The Heritage Lottery Fund (HLF) announced it had awarded the final stage of the £1,778,000 grant to the Arcadia project to the Borough of Richmond-upon-Thames to help revitalise the riverside landscape stretching from Richmond Lock to Twickenham.

In 2005 the Rugby Football Union started work on a two-year, £80m project to build a new South Stand, which will increase the ground's capacity from 75,000 to 82,500, and fully enclose the playing area to make

MARBLE HILL HOUSE 2004 ZZZ05252

Marble Hill House seen from the opposite bank of the Thames, after shrub clearance opened up the view.

ARCADIA IN THE CITY

'Arcadia in the City' is a £2.5m package for enhancing the landscape, access, and nature conservation on and below the brow of Richmond Hill, and to restore and conserve the landscape beside the Thames as it flows through Twickenham. The strategy's objective is to regenerate and manage the many historic buildings, landscaped gardens, avenues and meadowlands through 122 projects over four years.

TWICKENHAM MUSEUM

Efforts to establish a museum for Twickenham stemmed from the creation of the Museum of Richmond. The matter was first raised at the AGM of the Borough of Twickenham Local History Society in 1986, and the first proposal was that the museum should occupy part of the stables behind Orleans House Gallery. In 1988 a working party was formed with representatives from local societies to move the project forward. In 1991 an exhibition was held at the gallery entitled 'A Museum for Twickenham?' This received strong public support and, in 1993, the working party was formalized as an independent charity.

In 1994 Jack Ellis died; he was a long-time member of the Twickenham Society, and left his estate to the trustees of the charity; this included his house at 25 The Embankment. The trustees resolved to establish the museum there because of uncertainty about the future of Orleans House Gallery. Extended litigation delayed possession until 1999, and the house was gradually emptied of its contents.

Open Days were held in 2000, and small displays mounted. Plans were drawn up for major conversion work, which was completed during 2001. The Museum opened fully in 2002 for regular exhibitions. It maintains a comprehensive web site about the history of the town at www. twickenham-museum.org.uk.

TWICKENHAM MUSEUM 2005 T91721k
(Hazelle Jackson)

a complete bowl. The RFU is also building a 156-bed, 4-star Marriott hotel including six VIP suites with views over the pitch, conference and exhibition space; a 400-seat performing arts centre; a Virgin Active health and fitness club; office space for the RFU; and a new Rugby Store. The demolition of the previous South Stand took place on 10 July 2005 when residents were allowed to view the controlled explosion from the safety of the A316.

Twickenham may lack the glamour of Richmond but it is older and tougher than its more sophisticated neighbour. Hidden away down side streets and tucked between dull modern developments, its residents enjoy a unique blend of art, architecture and community pride distilled from over 1,000 years of history. The town looks backward with pride and affection at its historic past and forward with optimism to its future.

A VIEW OF THE RIVER 2005 T91722k (Hazelle Jackson)

THE THAMES WATERFRONT AT LOW TIDE 2005 ZZZ05267 (Hazelle Jackson)

TWICKENHAM'S COAT OF ARMS

The Y-shaped crossing, or pall, symbolises the name of Twickenham (the place where the two ways meet), and also the close historical connection with the see of Canterbury. The lamp stands for the town's interest in literature, the arts and the sciences represented by such distinguished citizens as Bacon, Dickens, Tennyson, Pope, Walpole and Turner. The crossed swords, taken from the see of London, refer to the earliest record of Twickenham when the land in the manor of Isleworth was granted to Waldhere, Bishop of London in 704. The three red roses are from the arms of the educational pioneer William of Wykeham, who was believed to have been responsible for the building of St Mary's Church tower.

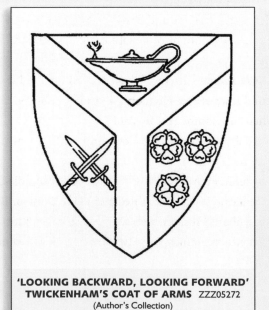

**'LOOKING BACKWARD, LOOKING FORWARD'
TWICKENHAM'S COAT OF ARMS** ZZZ05272
(Author's Collection)

ACKNOWLEDGEMENTS

Jane Baxter, local studies librarian, and staff at the Local Studies Collection,

London Borough of Richmond-upon-Thames.

The volunteers at Twickenham Museum.

Twickenham Local History Society.

Contributors to the Twickenham Museum's web site.

The York House Society.

The Friends of Turner's House.

The Twickenham Society.

The Twickenham Riverside Terrace Group.

Twickenham Online website.

The London Borough of Richmond-upon-Thames.

FURTHER READING

'Twickenham Past' by Donald Simpson, Historical Publications, 1993.

'Twickenham 1600-1900 People and Places', Borough of Twickenham Local History Society Paper Number 47, reprinted 1984.

'Twickenham and Isleworth in the Domesday Book 1086', A C B Urwin, Borough of Twickenham Local History Society Paper 34, 1976.

'Isleworth - a Guide and Some of its History', Isleworth Community Council, 1991.

'Middlesex County Council - a Jubilee Year Guide 1889-1939', C W Radcliffe, Evans Brothers Limited, 1939.

'Twickenham As It Was' - written and compiled by the Borough of Twickenham Local History Society, second impression, Hendon Publishing, May 1976.

'When the Bombs Fell' by Paul Barnfield, the Borough of Twickenham Local History Society, 2001.

'The Rabbit Warrens of Twickenham', A C B Urwin, Borough of Twickenham Local History Society, Paper 58, 1986.

'Twickenham: A History of the County of Middlesex: Volume III', Victoria County History series, c/o Institute of Historical Research, University of London.

Twickenham Museum web site: www.twickenham-museum.org.uk

Twickenham Online: www.twickenham-online.co.uk

Francis Frith
Pioneer Victorian Photographer

Francis Frith, founder of the world-famous photographic archive, was a complex and multi-talented man. A devout Quaker and a highly successful Victorian businessman, he was philosophical by nature and pioneering in outlook. By 1855 he had already established a wholesale grocery business in Liverpool, and sold it for the astonishing sum of £200,000, which is the equivalent today of over £15,000,000. Now in his thirties, and captivated by the new science of photography, Frith set out on a series of pioneering journeys up the Nile and to the Near East.

He was the first photographer to venture beyond the sixth cataract of the Nile. Africa was still the mysterious 'Dark Continent', and Stanley and Livingstone's historic meeting was a decade into the future. The conditions for picture taking confound belief. He laboured for hours in his wicker dark-room in the sweltering heat of the desert, while the volatile chemicals fizzed dangerously in their trays. Back in London he exhibited his photographs and was 'rapturously cheered' by members of the Royal Society. His reputation as a photographer was made overnight.

By the 1870s the railways had threaded their way across the country, and Bank Holidays and half-day Saturdays had been made obligatory by Act of Parliament. All of a sudden the working man and his family were able to enjoy days out, take holidays, and see a little more of the world.

With typical business acumen, Francis Frith foresaw that these new tourists would enjoy having souvenirs to commemorate their days out. For the next thirty years he travelled the country by train and by pony and trap, producing fine photographs of seaside resorts and beauty spots that were keenly bought by millions of Victorians. These prints were painstakingly pasted into family albums and pored over during the dark nights of winter, rekindling precious memories of summer excursions. Frith's studio was soon supplying retail shops all over the country, and by 1890 F Frith & Co had become the greatest specialist photographic publishing company in the world, with over 2,000 sales outlets, and pioneered the picture postcard.

Francis Frith had died in 1898 at his villa in Cannes, his great project still growing. By 1970 the archive he created contained over a third of a million pictures showing 7,000 British towns and villages.

Frith's legacy to us today is of immense significance and value, for the magnificent archive of evocative photographs he created provides a unique record of change in the cities, towns and villages throughout Britain over a century and more. Frith and his fellow studio photographers revisited locations many times down the years to update their views, compiling for us an enthralling and colourful pageant of British life and character.

We are fortunate that Frith was dedicated to recording the minutiae of everyday life. For it is this sheer wealth of visual data, the painstaking chronicle of changes in dress, transport, street layouts, buildings, housing and landscape that captivates us so much today, offering us a powerful link with the past and with the lives of our ancestors.

Computers have now made it possible for Frith's many thousands of images to be accessed almost instantly. The archive offers every one of us an opportunity to examine the places where we and our families have lived and worked down the years. Its images, depicting our shared past, are now bringing pleasure and enlightenment to millions around the world a century and more after his death. For further information visit: www.francisfrith.co.uk

FREE PRINT OF YOUR CHOICE

Mounted Print
Overall size 14 x 11 inches (355 x 280mm)

Choose any Frith photograph in this book. Please note: photographs with a reference number starting with a "Z" are not Frith photographs and cannot be supplied under this offer.

Simply complete the Voucher opposite and return it with your remittance for £2.25 (to cover postage and handling) and we will print the photograph of your choice in SEPIA (size 11 x 8 inches) and supply it in a cream mount with a burgundy rule line (overall size 14 x 11 inches). **Offer valid for delivery to one UK address only.**

PLUS: **Order additional Mounted Prints at HALF PRICE - £7.49 each** (normally £14.99)
If you would like to order more Frith prints from this book, possibly as gifts for friends and family, you can buy them at half price (with no additional postage and handling costs).

PLUS: **Have your Mounted Prints framed**
For an extra £14.95 per print you can have your mounted print(s) framed in an elegant polished wood and gilt moulding, overall size 16 x 13 inches (no additional postage and handling required).

IMPORTANT!

These special prices are only available if you use this form to order. You must use the ORIGINAL VOUCHER on this page (no copies permitted). We can only despatch to one UK address. This offer cannot be combined with any other offer.

Send completed Voucher form to:
The Francis Frith Collection, Frith's Barn, Teffont, Salisbury, Wiltshire SP3 5QP

CHOOSE A PHOTOGRAPH FROM THIS BOOK

Voucher for FREE and Reduced Price Frith Prints

Please do not photocopy this voucher. Only the original is valid, so please fill it in, cut it out and return it to us with your order.

Picture ref no	Page no	Qty	Mounted @ £7.49	Framed + £14.95	Total Cost £
		1	Free of charge*	£	£
			£7.49	£	£
			£7.49	£	£
			£7.49	£	£
			£7.49	£	£
			£7.49	£	£

Please allow 28 days for delivery. Offer available to one UK address only

* Post & handling	£2.25
Total Order Cost	£

Title of this book . . . .

I enclose a cheque/postal order for £ . . . .
made payable to 'The Francis Frith Collection'

OR please debit my Mastercard / Visa / Maestro / Amex card, details below

Card Number

Issue No (Maestro only)   Valid from (Maestro)

Expires   Signature

Name Mr/Mrs/Ms . . . .
Address . . . .
. . . .
. . . .
. . . . Postcode . . . .
Daytime Tel No . . . .
Email . . . .

ISBN: 1-84589-220-8   Valid to 31/12/08

FREE PRINT - SEE OVERLEAF

CAN YOU HELP US WITH INFORMATION ABOUT ANY OF THE FRITH PHOTOGRAPHS IN THIS BOOK?

We are gradually compiling an historical record for each of the photographs in the Frith archive. It is always fascinating to find out the names of the people shown in the pictures, as well as insights into the shops, buildings and other features depicted.

If you recognize anyone in the photographs in this book, or if you have information not already included in the author's caption, do let us know. We would love to hear from you, and will try to publish it in future books or articles.

OUR PRODUCTION TEAM

Frith books are produced by a small dedicated team at offices in the converted Grade II listed 18th-century barn at Teffont near Salisbury, illustrated above. Most have worked with the Frith Collection for many years. All have in common one quality: they have a passion for the Frith Collection. The team is constantly expanding, but currently includes:

Paul Baron, Jason Buck, John Buck, Heather Crisp, David Davies, Louis du Mont, Isobel Hall, Lucy Hart, Julian Hight, Peter Horne, James Kinnear, Karen Kinnear, Tina Leary, Stuart Login, Sue Molloy, Miles Murray, Sarah Roberts, Kate Rotondetto, Dean Scource, Eliza Sackett, Terence Sackett, Sandra Sampson, Adrian Sanders, Sandra Sanger, Julia Skinner, Lewis Taylor, Shelley Tolcher, Lorraine Tuck, Miranda Tunnicliffe, David Turner and Ricky Williams.